From the Author

"Hi, there! My name is Ashish Singh, and I am from a very humble background from the eastern parts of Uttar Pradesh. After completing college in 2007, I came to Mumbai and started working in the IT industry. Since I had an interest in the Indian stock market and how it works, I started reading about it.

Gradually, I heard about derivatives trading, started reading about it, and was completely awestruck with all the permutation and combinations it offers a trader. Since I had the cushion of a job to financially support my passion, I started trading after the 2008 market crash. Markets were in a recovery mode at that time, so buying options gave me good profits but the real lessons — read, losses — and dynamics I learnt when the markets were stagnant in 2010. Through this book, I am sharing with you my decade-long experience and learnings of options trading.

~

MAKING MONEY BY SELLING OPTIONS

– SIMPLIFIED

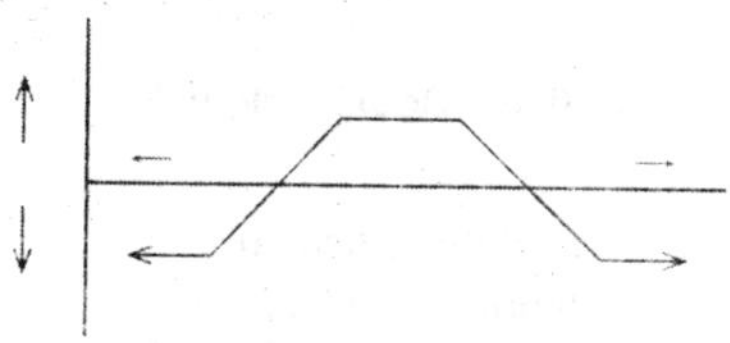

ASHISH SINGH

VISION BOOKS

www.visionbooksindia.com

www.visionbooksindia.com

Disclaimer

Investing and trading invariably involve some risk. The author and the publisher disclaim all legal or other responsibilities for any losses which readers may suffer by investing or trading based on information provided in this book, which is meant only for educational purpose. Readers are advised to seek professional advice and guidance before making any trades or investments.

A Vision Books Original

First Published 2022
Reprinted 2023, 2024

ISBN 10: 93-86268-61-2
ISBN 13: 978-93-86268-61-7

Published by
Vision Books Pvt. Ltd.
(Incorporating Orient Paperbacks and CARING imprints)
24 Feroze Gandhi Road, Lajpat Nagar 3
New Delhi 110024, India.
Phone: (+91-11) 2984 0821 / 22
e-mail: visionbooks@gmail.com

Printed at
Ashim Print Line
38/2, 35 &36 Sahibabad Industrial Area, Ghaziabad
Uttar Pradesh 201010, India.

Dedication

~

To my better half, Kumud,
who inspired me to write this book.
And
for our daughter, Nandini.

"Never spend your money before you have earned it."

— *Thomas Jefferson*

Contents

~

Preface

This book is not an extensive treatise on derivatives and options. Rather, I have confined myself to providing knowledge and guidance that is essential for an individual investor to become a successful options trader.

In other words, this book has been written for those relatively new to options trading.

The main aim of this book is to steer you towards the right path in becoming a successful options trader, without bombarding you with unnecessary technical jargon which often floats about in the world of derivatives. In my early days of trading, I acutely felt the lack of good books which could guide me in my trading in simple terms, teach me the essentials of what I needed to know, rather than all that there is to know.

Derivative market scenarios, strategies, and terminology can be unending. Unless you are clear on what you need to know, you will get lost even before you start any actual trading.

This book focuses on providing you sufficient and relevant knowledge and guidance to get you started in options trading. Thereafter, the best teacher will be your own trading experience. You will learn more from real-life trading, with all its ups and downs, than any book can teach you.

In this book we will also look at how you can form your own perspective about the market. We will then move on to option Greeks, and to various option selling strategies which are suitable for individual traders. I have also tried to summarize key points related to options trading which I have learned over a decade of trading. I have only described those concepts that a trader truly needs to become successful in his or her trading journey and avoid the mistakes that new traders always make.

Along with tactics of trading, I have also focused on the behavioral aspect which one needs to inculcate in order to have a prolonged and successful trading journey.

A singular highlight of this book is the discussion about how you can adjust your ongoing option trades in case the market moves adversely *vis-a-vis* your original trade set-up.

Another highlight is the detailed analysis of my own real life trades, alongwith the complete logic and rationale behind those trades. I hope these examples will help you learn why some trades succeeded, while others failed.

Finally, the book provides a concise roadmap for making consistent income from options trading, month after month. If I can do it, so can you.

Introduction

~

Who doesn't like money? I do, too.

Why I Started Trading

It's said that if you want to become a millionaire, then you should have seven (!) sources of income. As a regular IT guy with a full day job, and household chores to help out with, if I were to think about other sources of income, there could be the following possibilities:

1. Salary at the end of every month.
   And, after a lot of thinking . . .
2. I could try to become a social media sensation and bombard my pictures, along perhaps with those of my pet, on Facebook or Instagram and hope that some company or the other might sponsor my pet and I. But the big question is: who would like to see a middle-aged man in his pyjamas?
3. I could attempt to become a YouTuber and try to post videos of my travels and hope to earn money through advertisements. But I don't think my boss would be lenient enough to give me generous leave on a regular basis!

4. I could become a technology trainer. But in order to teach I first need to learn and refresh my knowledge in order to be well versed with current tech trends. Too much effort: let's skip it!
5. Become a motivational speaker, perhaps? I believe that not everyone should aspire to become one, especially a not-so-much-motivated person like me.
6. A full-time second job after office hours? But this is neither legally allowed nor would many people have the energy to spend eighteen hours a day in office. So, this is also crossed out.
7. Dividend and interest income from stocks and fixed deposits? This could be an option, but to earn a handsome interest you need to have a big fixed deposit, or a large equity investment corpus. Most people, including me, have neither.

From the above list, I am not sure about the other five sources of income but my salary, and monthly income from options trading are the two sources that I can count on.

What this Book Contains

This book explains the essential concepts and strategies that are required for trading options. We will start with an understanding of the basic mindset needed for trading, and then move to essential concepts relating to options.

Once we understand option Greeks, we will discuss a few prominent trading strategies which you can use, irrespective of whether your view of the market is bearish, bullish, or neutral. There is also some specialist terminology related to options which we will describe and explore.

Typically, most trading books stop at this point. In this book, however, we will go further and learn how to adjust your trade if it starts to go wrong mid-way. This will be your big edge in de-risking options trading. To strengthen your understanding, I have also included some of my actual trades in this book, with all necessary details, including my thinking process, trade execution and trade adjustments.

Towards the end of the book, we will create a roadmap for earning monthly income through options.

Note:
Please note that the lot sizes and trading rules mentioned in this book are as of the fourth quarter of 2020. Since National Stock Exchange of India (NSE) keeps changing rules and lot sizes from time to time, please refer to https://www.nseindia.com/ for the latest information.

1

~

Basics of Derivatives

In this chapter we will look at what derivatives, are and what their different types.

There now exists on the Internet and business channels a mountain of information about the derivatives market and about trading derivatives. It is such a vast field that even those who have been trading for two or more decades can't claim complete knowledge. So unless you navigate your journey very carefully, you can easily be overwhelmed, and even put off, from options trading. Thereafter you may either lose interest in trading altogether, or go back to stock trading, which is conventionally considered a safer bet than trading derivatives.

Without further ado, let me now introduce you to the derivatives market in India; and from there we will proceed to explore all that you need to learn for the purpose of earning a regular monthly income by trading options.

What Derivatives Are

In simple terms, a derivative is an instrument high or contract based on, and deriving its value from another underlying asset or instrument.

The most widely traded derivative in India is Nifty50 which is based on the popular Nifty index made up of 50 Indian stocks. The highly volatile derivative BankNifty is based on the Bank Nifty index, which is made up of 12 liquid and well capitalized stocks from the banking sector.

The derivatives of Nifty and BankNifty are called index derivatives, since their underlying instruments are indices.

Then there are stock derivatives, too. For example, 1,000 shares of Reliance Industries Ltd. (RIL) constitute one lot of the Reliance stock derivative. In the case of State Bank of India (SBI), 3,000 shares constitute a single lot of SBI derivative. In the case of HDFC Bank, 550 shares constitute one derivative lot*. Stock derivatives are comparatively more volatile than index derivatives.

In India, stock derivatives and index derivatives are both traded on the National Stock Exchange (NSE).

---

* See note on page 16.

Underlying Asset / Instrument

As of 2020, futures contracts were available on 172 Indian securities stipulated by the Securities & Exchange Board of India (SEBI). These securities are traded in the capital market segment of the stock exchange. Apart from these 172 securities, there are Index Futures based on various indices such as Nifty50, NiftyBank, Nifty IT index, etc.

With this basic understanding clear, let's now move on to the two different types of derivatives:

1. Futures; and
2. Options.

Futures Contracts

A futures contract is an agreement to buy, or sell, an underlying asset at a pre-determined future date for a pre-determined price.

By purchasing the right to buy, an investor expects to profit from an increase in the underlying asset's price during the life of the contract.

By purchasing the right to sell, on the other hand, the trader expects to profit from a fall in the price of the underlying asset during the life of the contract.

Futures trades are directional trades.

Directional trades are those where traders make money by betting correctly on the market's future direction. If your view of the market's direction turns out to be correct, you make money; if your view turns out to be wrong, you will lose money.

Option Contracts

An option is a derivative contract that gives the buyer the right, without imposing an obligation or compulsion to do so, to buy or sell the underlying asset by a certain date, called the expiration date, at the price specified in the contract, known as the strike price.

With options, too, you can make money by correctly betting on the market's future direction, just as you do with futures.

In addition, options also provide profitable trade opportunity for non-directional trades. Non-directional trades are those where a trader makes money irrespective of the direction of the market movement. In simpler terms, non-directional trades do not react to small changes in the price of the underlying stock or index. Whether the underlying stock goes up or down, a non-directional trade position maintains its value which neither increases nor falls.

Types of Options

Options are of two types:

- Call options; and
- Put options.

Call options are bought if the trader expects the price of the underlying asset to rise within a certain time frame.

On the other hand, **call options are sold** if the trader expects the price of the underlying asset to fall within a certain time frame.

Put options are bought if the trader expects the price of the underlying asset to fall within a certain time frame.

On the other hand, **put options are sold** if the trader expects the price of the underlying asset to increase within a certain time frame.

We will see the dynamics and workings all these later in this book.

Settlement of Options

Option settlement is the process by which the respective obligations of the buyer and seller of an options contract are settled after the contract is exercised.

Each options trade, whether a buy trade or a sell trade, has to be marked to market (MTM; more on this in Chapter 5), and profits or losses from the trade are earmarked to the accounts of the parties to the trade.

Premiums need to be collected from option buyers, while margins are collected from option sellers. All these activities fall under the process called options settlement.

There are two types of options settlement:

1. American style, and
2. European style.

American style options can be exercised at any time prior to their expiration.

European style options, on the other hand, can only be exercised on their fixed expiration date.

In India, we follow European style options settlement for both index options and stock options.

Since the buyer of an option receives a privilege, s/he pays a fee, called option premium, for receiving this privilege.

On the other hand, since the seller of the option accepts an obligation, s/he receives a fee, namely the option premium, for doing so.

The premium is the price negotiated and settled when the option is bought or sold.

A person who buys an option is said to be "long" in the option.

The person who sells, or writes, an option is said to be "short" in the option.

Trading Cycle

In India, futures contracts are presently available in three different trading cycles:

1. First, the near-month contract, which is of one-month duration;
2. Second, the next-month contract, which is of two-month duration; and
3. Third, the far-month contract of three-month duration.

Once the ongoing cycle of any of the above contracts expires, the next trading cycle of contracts are introduced for all the three trading cycles. In this way, there are always be 3 contracts available for trading in the market for each security at any time, i.e. one a near-month contract, second a mid-month or next month contract, and the third a far-month contract for a 3-month duration, respectively.

Expiry Day

In India, all option contracts expire on the last Thursday of the expiry month. If the last Thursday is a trading holiday, the contracts expire on the previous trading day.

Margin Money

Before proceeding any further, we need to understand what margin money, or margin, is.

Margin is the money that a trader has to deposit with his broker, or an exchange, to cover the credit risk his trade could conceivably pose for the broker or the exchange.

In the case of futures contracts, margin is the amount of money that you must deposit in your brokerage account in order to honor and fulfill any obligations that you may incur by trading futures contracts. Such margin is required by your broker since he would need money to be able to cover, or pay, for your losses if a futures trade goes wrong for you. The status of traded futures contracts are updated at the end of each trading day, and you may be required to put in additional funds into your account if your trade had moved against you on that day.

The initial sum you must deposit in your brokerage account to cover your position is known as the **initial margin,** and any subsequent sum you have to add to the account is known as **maintenance margin,** or exposure margin.

Later in the book we will see how these margins are calculated by the exchange.

In options trading, too, margin is very similar to what it means in futures trading because it too is an amount of money that you must put into your account with your broker. This money is required when you write contracts, i.e. sell options, to cover any potential liability which you may incur during the trade. This is because whenever you write option contracts you are essentially exposed to potentially unquantifiable, even unlimited, risk. On the other hand, since buying options doesn't involve unlimited risk, margin money is not required when you buy options. **The fact that buying options doesn't require margin money is the reason why many individual traders prefer to buy, rather than sell, options.**

Futures and Options Contracts in a Nutshell

Let's now strengthen our basic understanding of futures and options with the help of a summarized comparison encapsulated in Table 1.1.

Table 1.1

Futures and Options Contracts in a Nutshell

	Options		*Futures*
	Buying Options	*Selling Options*	
Obligation	Option buyer is not obligated to sell the underlying as he covers his risk by paying a premium, i.e. an advance amount, when entering into an options contract.	Option seller, on the other hand, is obligated to buy the underlying as he receives a premium, i.e. an amount in advance, when entering into an options contract.	Futures buyers and sellers are both obligated to buy and sell, respectively the underlying at the agreed price.
Money Requirement	Option buyer pays the full premium up front. However, his / her money requirement is comparatively much lower than if s/he were either to buy futures or sell options. That is because there is no margin money required for buying options.	Option seller receives the premium paid by the option buyer. The exchange retains the margin money deposited by the option seller till the time the trade is concluded.	Futures trading requires a relatively higher amount of margin money. The futures buyer doesn't have to pay any money in advance. The money is blocked by the exchange till the trade is concluded.
Profit	Unlimited profit potential.	Profit is limited to the premium received.	Unlimited profit potential.
Loss	Limited loss.	Unlimited loss possibility.	Unlimited loss possibility.
Risk	Risk is limited to the premium paid.	High risk.	High risk.
Trade Execution	Trade execution (exercise) can happen on any date before the expiry.	Trade execution (exercise) can happen on any date before the expiry.	Trade execution can happen on any date before the expiry.

2

~

Option Terminology, the Option Chain and Open Interest

As described in Chapter 1, an option is a derivative, a contract that gives a trader the right, but not the obligation, to buy the underlying asset by a certain date, called the expiration date, at a specified price, called the strike price.

Two Types of Options

There are two types of options:

- Call options; and
- Put options.

A call option gives a trader the right to buy at the strike price, on or before the expiration date.

A put option gives a trader the right to sell at a specific price on or before the expiry of the contract.

Options Terminology

A proper understanding of the terminology related to derivatives is very important. Since we are focusing on options trading, let's understand the relevant options terminology.

We will discuss the option terminology, option chain, and open interest (OI) with the help of the September 2020 series.

Option Chain

Go to https://www.nseindia.com/ in your browser and search for 'NIFTY'. Then go to the derivatives tab and there you will see the 'Expiry Date' dropdown. Select any date, and you would see an option chain like the one shown in Table 2.1.

Let's now look at the different sections of this option chain.

Strike Price

This is the price per share of the underlying asset / instrument at which the option can be exercised, i.e., bought or sold. The strike price is listed in the middle column of the option chain.

Table 2.1

~

A Nifty Option Chain

					CALLS										PUTS					
OI	CHNG IN OI	Volume	IV	LTP	CHNG	BID Qty	BID Price	ASK Price	ASK Qty	STRIKE Price	BID Qty	BID Price	ASK Price	ASK Qty	CHNG	LTP	IV	Volume	CHNG IN OI	OI
522	131	311	28.49	**441.75**	-123.55	675	411.20	416.10	75	**11,100**	1,725	14.65	14.80	1,350	6.10	**14.75**	30.45	74,883	-1,650	10,940
149	115	235	32.86	**365.00**	-162.75	600	365.00	365.50	375	**11,150**	300	17.40	17.55	1,275	7.45	**17.40**	29.20	21,305	120	3,005
850	-29	584	32.63	**317.00**	-152.50	375	319.50	321.80	150	**11,200**	750	21.45	21.60	75	9.90	**21.50**	37.94	1,51,587	1,098	18,445
92	56	139	30.56	**275.00**	-148.40	75	276.55	278.95	75	**11,250**	150	27.35	27.50	600	13.85	**27.45**	26.84	38.823	-35	5,939
1,908	-522	3,119	29.10	**234.25**	-141.35	75	234.55	236.40	150	**11,300**	375	36.40	36.60	150	20.10	**36.50**	26.17	2,34,165	748	22,536
264	-2	465	26.63	**195.05**	-133.55	75	195.15	197.00	375	**11,350**	150	47.15	47.45	150	27.60	**47.40**	25.33	89,422	-1,363	6,451
3,754	-103	7,160	27.23	**159.60**	-123.15	75	159.05	159.90	75	**11,400**	450	61.25	61.65	600	36.75	**61.50**	24.55	2,95,117	-851	23,926
1,864	93	2,198	26.54	**128.40**	-111.35	75	128.20	128.95	75	**11,450**	225	78.90	79.30	150	47.95	**78.65**	23.80	1,15,585	-470	7,677
18,390	4,363	52,770	25.54	**99.65**	-98.10	75	99.35	99.70	1,650	**11,500**	75	100.60	101.00	600	61.25	**100.35**	23.16	4,52,957	-2,479	34,286
5,436	3,499	39,974	24.87	**76.20**	-82.30	150	76.00	76.20	75	**11,550**	150	126.50	127.00	75	77.70	**127.00**	22.50	1,80,632	2,711	10,594
31,314	13,816	2,26,286	24.47	**57.80**	-64.40	225	57.60	57.80	75	**11,600**	150	158.00	158.65	75	94.60	**157.80**	22.01	4,55,108	-6,637	28,407
12,018	3,939	1,17,937	24.07	**42.35**	-48.70	75	42.20	42.40	600	**11,650**	75	191.20	192.35	225	110.60	**192.35**	21.30	1,52,209	-2,954	3,771
33,066	11,511	3,73,239	23.89	**30.65**	-33.80	225	30.55	30.70	450	**11,700**	75	231.40	232.00	75	125.70	**230.85**	20.82	3,09,234	1,941	10,185
15,934	3,907	2,05,135	23.88	**22.40**	-20.65	225	22.25	22.40	1,800	**11,750**	300	270.75	272.05	75	137.40	**271.45**	19.97	99,558	1,129	2,052
42,143	18,274	4,95,617	23.89	**15.80**	-11.40	450	15.80	15.90	225	**11,800**	75	316.95	318.25	75	150.00	**316.30**	19.82	1,23,949	1,873	4,099
14,707	3,133	1,82,362	24.10	**11.35**	-4.85	75	11.30	11.40	1,875	**11,850**	75	360.90	362.75	75	154.25	**360.50**	19.56	13,306	137	472
32,827	11,198	3,72,215	24.56	**8.50**	-1.25	8,550	8.40	8.45	1,875	**11,900**	75	409.45	410.50	150	159.65	**409.85**	-	22,857	510	1,085
9,950	1,191	1,23,271	25.12	**6.20**	0.05	1,200	6.15	6.25	2,100	**11,950**	150	455.85	461.15	75	161.45	**459.40**	34.23	476	84	150
43,069	9,895	3,17,814	26.16	**4.95**	0.50	1,800	4.95	5.00	16,200	**12,000**	225	504.45	507.10	75	161.80	**504.55**	-	5,364	231	1,122

Call (CE)

As we noted, call is an option contract that gives a trader the right to buy the underlying at the defined strike price. You can see the various available call options (calls) on the left side of the strike price column in Table 2.1.

Put (PE)

Put is an option contract that gives a trader the right to sell the underlying at the defined strike price. You can see the various available puts on the right side of the strike price column in Table 2.1.

Last Traded Price (LTP)

This is the price (premium) a trader pays for buying an option, or receives upon selling an option.

For example, if you see the Nifty Option Chain in Table 2.1, the 11,800 CE option is trading at ₹15.80. The lot size of Nifty is 75. From a call option buyer's perspective, one needs to spend 75 × ₹15.80 = ₹1,185 to buy a call option of Nifty 11,800.

In turn, the option seller will receive the same ₹1,185 as premium for selling a call option of Nifty 11,800.

We will look at the various components of the option premium a little later in this chapter under the heading, 'Option Premium or Option Price'.

At-the-Money Option (ATM)

An option is said to be at-the-money (ATM) if the market price of the underlying is equal to the option's strike price. Thus, for example, if Nifty is trading at 11,500, then the 11,500 option strike will be an ATM strike.

In-the-Money Option (ITM)

- A call option is said to be in-the-money (ITM) when the underlying's price is higher than the option's strike price. For example, if Nifty is trading at 11,500, then the 11,400 call strike will be an ITM strike.
- A put option, on the other hand, is said to be in-the-money (ITM) when the underlying's price is lower than the strike price. For example, if Nifty is trading at 11,500 then the 11,600 put strike will be an ITM strike.

Out-of-the-Money (OTM) Option

- A call option is out-of-the-money (OTM) when the underlying's price is lower than the strike price. For example, if Nifty is trading at 11,500 then the 11,600 call strike will be an OTM strike.

- A put option is said to be OTM when the underlying's price is higher than the strike price. For example, if Nifty is trading at 11,500, then the 11,400 put strike will be an OTM strike.

Open Interest (OI)

Open interest is the number of contracts bought or sold for a particular strike price. OI position can be found at the extreme right and left columns, respectively, of the option chain in Table 2.1.

Open interest also reveals the market sentiment. If the underlying stock or index price rise is accompanied by an increase in OI, the sentiment is bullish. Basically, this demonstrates that traders are making fresh position, translating into an increase in OI, in the expectation of prices going up further from current levels.

On the other hand, if the underlying's price falls and OI decreases, the sentiment is bearish. Such a situation would suggest that more and more traders are closing their positions, resulting in a reduction in OI on the expectation of the underlying prices to go down further.

Change in OI

Adjacent to the open interest (OI) column, there is the column "Change in OI" which shows the number of contracts added, or wound up, by traders that day for the particular strike price.

Implied Volatility (IV)

Implied volatility is the market's forecast of the likely future fluctuation of the underlying stock's or index's price.

Higher implied volatility suggests that the underlying's price is likely to fluctuate more – and this, in turn, results in its option commanding higher premium — and *vice versa*.

Trading Lot, or Lot

Trading lot is the number of shares of the underlying that constitutes a single derivative trading unit, called a trading lot. In derivatives trading, you can only trade in lots, whether a single lot or multiple lots; you cannot trade just a single share, or any arbitrary number of shares, of the underlying instrument.

For example, as of July 2020 the lot size of Nifty for derivatives trading was 75, for Bank Nifty it was 25, for HDFC Bank it was 550, and so on. A trader can buy or sell calls or puts only in a multiple of the relevant lot size.

Expiry of Derivatives

Every derivative has an expiry date. As the name suggests, it is the date when the concerned option contract expires; namely, it is the date after which the right to buy or sell stands extinguished.

The expiry date is of three types:

- It may be the current month's expiry, which is the last Thursday of the current month.
- It may be the near-month expiry which would be the last Thursday of the next month.
- It may be far-month expiry which will be the last Thursday of the month after the next.

Say, we are in the month of July YYYY, then July YYYY will be the current month, August YYYY will be the near month, and September YYYY will be the far month. Expiry would happen on the last Thursday of each of the three months.

Enter Weekly Expiry

In 2019, SEBI introduced weekly expiry contracts for indices like Nifty and Bank Nifty. Expiry of weekly options occurs on Thursday of each week. The last Thursday of each month therefore now has two expiries for Nifty and Bank Nifty derivatives — monthly expiry and weekly expiry.

No weekly expiry contracts are allowed for individual stocks as of 2020.

Breakeven Point

This is the price point above which you will start to lose money in the case of a put option (PE) — or earn money in the case of a call option (CE).

For example, let's assume that you have purchased a Nifty call option of 11,500 strike at an option premium of ₹50. Since you are the buyer of the call option, you will earn money if Nifty moves up quickly. For you as the buyer, the breakeven price will be 11,550, namely the strike price, plus the option premium paid. Thus, only if Nifty moves above 11,550, would you be in profit as the CE buyer.

On the other hand, if you are a seller of the Nifty 11,500 strike option at an option premium of ₹50 then you will earn money if the Nifty stays below the 11,550 level, namely the strike price plus the option premium received. In this case, the breakeven point will be 11,550. If the market moves above 11,550, the option seller will start to lose money.

Risk Reward Ratio

Before initiating any trade, you should work out its risk-reward ratio. This is the ratio of the amount of capital you are willing to risk for a certain reward. Suppose in an options trade you expect to collect a premium of ₹10,000. Now, if the maximum risk in the trade is ₹15,000, then the risk-reward ratio will be 1.5:1.

You might often have heard that options have the potential of unlimited profit; and can also have unlimited loss. In real life, however, you will not wait for your losses to mount exponentially. Instead, you will close the trade before it gets to unacceptable losses.

If you are selling options using a hedged multi-leg strategy, which will be explained later in the book, then the extent of risk is well defined.

In case you trade using a naked options strategy, to protect yourself from unacceptable losses you would need to place a stop loss in your trading terminal every day since the stop loss has only one-day validity.

Option Premium or Option Price

Option premium is the amount an option buyer pays to buy an option, and also the amount an option seller receives when s/he sells an option.

Option premium is made up of two components, namely:

- Intrinsic value, and
- Extrinsic value.

Intrinsic value reflects the actual, or existing, value inherent in the option were it to expire today. It arises from an interplay between the option's strike price and the underlying's current market price.

Extrinsic value, also known as time value, is determined by the time left till the option's expiration, implied volatility (IV) of the underlying asset, dividends, and the prevailing interest rates.

Intrinsic Value

The intrinsic value is different for call options and put options. Let's see how.

Intrinsic Value of a Call Option

A call option is said to be in-the-money (ITM) when the underlying security's price is higher than the option's strike price. Thus, suppose the SBI share is trading at ₹400, then the 380CE will be in-the-money and its intrinsic value will be as under:

> Intrinsic value of a call option = current price of the underlying SBI (₹400) – strike price of the option (₹380) = ₹20

Let's now calculate the intrinsic value for an out-of-the-money (OTM) call option. So let's find out what, for example, what would be the intrinsic value of the 410 call option of SBI if its share is currently trading at ₹400?

Intrinsic value = ₹ (400 – 410) = – ₹10

But since we know that the premium value can't be negative, hence it is considered to be 0.

In the case of at-the-money (ATM) options, too, the intrinsic value will be 0.

Intrinsic Value of a Put Option

A put option is in-the-money (ITM) if the underlying security's price is lower than the option's strike price.

For example, if the SBI share is trading at ₹380, then the 400PE will be in-the-money (ITM), and its intrinsic value will be as follows:

Intrinsic value of put option = Strike price of the option (₹400) – correct price of the security (₹380) = ₹20

What would be the intrinsic value of SBI's 370 put option if the share is currently trading at ₹380?

Intrinsic value = ₹370 – ₹380 = – ₹10.

But since the premium value can't be negative, hence it is considered to be 0. For at-the-money (ATM) options also, the intrinsic value will be 0.

Thus, as the above examples, show only in-the-money options, i.e. ITM options, have intrinsic value.

Extrinsic Value or Time Value

Time value is that portion of an option's premium which is in excess of its intrinsic value before expiration. Other factors being the same, the longer the period of time available before expiry, the higher would be the option's time value. At the time of expiry, time value becomes zero.

Time value = Option premium – Intrinsic value

To arrive at the time value of an option, whether a call option or a put option, you first need to calculate its intrinsic value, and then subtract that intrinsic value from the option's premium. Whatever is then left will be the option's time value.

Suppose, the SBI share is currently trading at ₹400, and the current premium for its 380 call option is ₹22. Then:

Intrinsic value = Current Price – Strike Price
= ₹400 – ₹380 = ₹20
Time value = Premium – Intrinsic value ₹ (22 – 20) = ₹2

So, ₹2 will be this option's time value.

Key Points to Remember about Option Premium

- Intrinsic value is the value available by exercising an in-the-money (ITM) option.

- At-the-money (ATM) options and out-of-the-money (OTM) options have no intrinsic value.
- At expiration, an option will only have intrinsic value, if any.
- OTM and ATM options have only extrinsic value, and no intrinsic value.

Option Sellers *versus* Option Buyers

- The buyer of a call option has the right, but is under no compulsion, to buy the underlying stock at the predetermined fixed price, i.e. the strike price.
- The seller of a call option, on the other hand, has the obligation to sell the underlying stock at the predetermined fixed price in case the buyer chooses to exercise his option to buy.
- The buyer of a put option has the right to sell the underlying stock at the predetermined fixed price, but is under no compulsion or obligation to do so.
- The seller of a put option, on the other hand, has the obligation to buy the underlying stock at the predetermined fixed price, namely the strike price, in case the option is exercised by the buyer.

In any ongoing trade clearly there has to be one party selling something and another party buying it.

Table 2.2

~

Nifty Option Chain

					CALLS										PUTS					
OI	CHNG IN OI	Volume	IV	**LTP**	CHNG	BID Qty	BID Price	ASK Price	ASK Qty	**STRIKE Price**	BID Qty	BID Price	ASK Price	ASK Qty	CHNG	**LTP**	IV	Volume	CHNG IN OI	OI
522	131	311	28.49	**441.75**	-123.55	675	411.20	416.10	75	**11,100**	1,725	14.65	14.80	1,350	6.10	**14.75**	30.45	74,883	-1,650	10,940
149	115	235	32.86	**365.00**	-162.75	600	365.00	365.50	375	**11,150**	300	17.40	17.55	1,275	7.45	**17.40**	29.20	21,305	120	3,005
850	-29	584	32.63	**317.00**	-152.50	375	319.50	321.80	150	**11,200**	750	21.45	21.60	75	9.90	**21.50**	37.94	1,51,587	1,098	18,445
92	56	139	30.56	**275.00**	-148.40	75	276.55	278.95	75	**11,250**	150	27.35	27.50	600	13.85	**27.45**	26.84	38.823	-35	5,939
1,908	-522	3,119	29.10	**234.25**	-141.35	75	234.55	236.40	150	**11,300**	375	36.40	36.60	150	20.10	**36.50**	26.17	2,34,165	748	22,536
264	-2	465	26.63	**195.05**	-133.55	75	195.15	197.00	375	**11,350**	150	47.15	47.45	150	27.60	**47.40**	25.33	89,422	-1,363	6,451
3,754	-103	7,160	27.23	**159.60**	-123.15	75	159.05	159.90	75	**11,400**	450	61.25	61.65	600	36.75	**61.50**	24.55	2,95,117	-851	23,926
1,864	93	2,198	26.54	**128.40**	-111.35	75	128.20	128.95	75	**11,450**	225	78.90	79.30	150	47.95	**78.65**	23.80	1,15,585	-470	7,677
18,390	4,363	52,770	25.54	**99.65**	-98.10	75	99.35	99.70	1,650	**11,500**	75	100.60	101.00	600	61.25	**100.35**	23.16	4,52,957	-2,479	34,286
5,436	3,499	39,974	24.87	**76.20**	-82.30	150	76.00	76.20	75	**11,550**	150	126.50	127.00	75	77.70	**127.00**	22.50	1,80,632	2,711	10,594
31,314	13,816	2,26,286	24.47	**57.80**	-64.40	225	57.60	57.80	75	**11,600**	150	158.00	158.65	75	94.60	**157.80**	22.01	4,55,108	-6,637	28,407
12,018	3,939	1,17,937	24.07	**42.35**	-48.70	75	42.20	42.40	600	**11,650**	75	191.20	192.35	225	110.60	**192.35**	21.30	1,52,209	-2,954	3,771
33,066	11,511	3,73,239	23.89	**30.65**	-33.80	225	30.55	30.70	450	**11,700**	75	231.40	232.00	75	125.70	**230.85**	20.82	3,09,234	1,941	10,185
15,934	3,907	2,05,135	23.88	**22.40**	-20.65	225	22.25	22.40	1,800	**11,750**	300	270.75	272.05	75	137.40	**271.45**	19.97	99,558	1,129	2,052
42,143	18,274	4,95,617	23.89	**15.80**	-11.40	450	15.80	15.90	225	**11,800**	75	316.95	318.25	75	150.00	**316.30**	19.82	1,23,949	1,873	4,099
14,707	3,133	1,82,362	24.10	**11.35**	-4.85	75	11.30	11.40	1,875	**11,850**	75	360.90	362.75	75	154.25	**360.50**	19.56	13,306	137	472
32,827	11,198	3,72,215	24.56	**8.50**	-1.25	8,550	8.40	8.45	1,875	**11,900**	75	409.45	410.50	150	159.65	**409.85**	-	22,857	510	1,085
9,950	1,191	1,23,271	25.12	**6.20**	0.05	1,200	6.15	6.25	2,100	**11,950**	150	455.85	461.15	75	161.45	**459.40**	34.23	476	84	150
43,069	9,895	3,17,814	26.16	**4.95**	0.50	1,800	4.95	5.00	16,200	**12,000**	225	504.45	507.10	75	161.80	**504.55**	-	5,364	231	1,122

Let's consider Table 2.2. Nifty is at 11,500. Now, if someone wants to buy an 11,700CE (call option), which is trading at ₹30.65, there has to be someone else willing to sell it for ₹30.65.

The Nifty lot size being 75, in order to buy a Nifty 11,700CE you will have to pay 75 × ₹30.65 = ₹2,298.75. If the market goes up from its current level of 11,500, the option premium of the 11,700CE will increase and the option buyer will be in profit.

On the other hand, option selling requires the seller to first deposit span and exposure margins. For example, to sell the same 11,700CE, the seller would need to deposit around ₹100,000 with his or her broker as a security deposit till the contract expires. Of course, the option seller will get to retain the premium, which is ₹2,298.75 in this case, but the requirement to deposit span and exposure margin money deters many traders from selling options.

On the other hand, since option buying involves only the cost of the premium and no margin money, most retail traders in India are option buyers and not option sellers.

Why Option Selling is More Profitable than Buying Options

You will find that large institutions almost always sell options, rarely buy them. Why is that so?

The reason is that, statistically, the chances of option sellers making money are 66%, while the chances of option buyers making money are only 33%.

Let us see how this is so.

Suppose Nifty is currently at 11,500. Now, by the time of expiry there could be one of the following three scenarios:

- Market may have fallen and the Nifty goes down to, say, 11,000. The probability of this happening is 33%.
- The market remains unchanged and expires at 11,500. The probability of this occurring is also 33%.
- There is a market rally and Nifty goes up to, say, 12,000. Again, the probability of this happening is 33%.

If I am an option seller and have sold the 11,500CE, it would mean that I am bearish about the market and I expect Nifty to close at or below 11,500. In this trade, I can lose money only when Nifty goes above 11,500 — and the probability of that occurring is only 33%, since it is only one of the three possible scenarios.

In the same way, if I have sold 11,500PE, it would suggest that I am bullish about the market and expect Nifty to close at, or above, 11,500. In other words, I can lose money only when Nifty goes below 11,500, and that's again a 33% probability.

Of course, option sellers can lose heavily when the market moves against them. That's especially true if you are selling naked options. That is the reason why in this book we strongly advise you to use only hedged strategies when selling options. Hedged option strategies afford you opportunities for appropriate adjustments in ongoing trades. They afford flexible protection to option sellers to turn losing trades into profitable ones, as we will see later. Stay tuned!

Summary

In this chapter we have discussed a few important concepts that you need to understand before you enter the world of options trading. From the next chapter on, we will discuss option Greeks and option trading strategies. The concepts discussed so far will help you grasp the trading strategies better. I would suggest that you read this chapter once again, if you feel you are not completely clear about these concepts.

3

~

Understanding Option Greeks

Option Greeks are an important concept in option trading because a change in an option's Greeks can, in turn, result in a change in the option's premium (price). The objective of this chapter is to explain Greeks in as clear a manner as possible.

Option premiums, i.e. the prices of options, are driven by multiple factors, including:

- Changes in the underlying's price;
- The passage of time;
- Changes in the expected volatility of the market or the underlying stock; and
- Changes in interest rates, etc.

In other words, option prices are sensitive to, i.e. affected by, these factors.

Collectively, these factors are called "the Greeks" because the symbols used to represent them come from calculus which uses Greek alphabets to denote various derivations.

Because Greeks measure the different factors that affect the price of an option, they provide traders a framework to assess their exposure to various factors that affect an option's price. This is the reason why Greeks are invaluable in making successful decisions in options trading. At the end of this chapter we will list some online resources available for calculating the various Greeks so that you can practice and validate the results of your own calculation. For now, let's first try and understand what the various Greeks are, and how they affect an option's premium.

Delta

Delta is the most important of all option Greeks. It is also the one which option sellers use all the time.

Delta measures how an option's premium, namely the option's price, changes with respect to a change in the underlying's price.

In other words, the Delta of an option provides the answer to the question: "By how many points will the option premium change for every one-point change in the underlying's price?"

The value of Delta ranges from –1 to 1.

- **Call options always have a positive Delta,** the value of which ranges from 0 to 1. This means that calls have a positive relationship with Delta and therefore the price of the underlying and the call option's price move in the same direction.

- **Put options, on the other hand, always have a negative Delta,** the value of which ranges from -1 to 0. This means that puts have a negative relationship with Delta. The negative Delta value of a put option indicates that the option's price and the underlying's price move in opposite directions to each other.
- Finally, **the closer Delta's value is to 1, the greater will be the move in the option's price when the underlying's price moves by 1.**

Assume we have a stock call option priced at ₹1.00, with a Delta of 0.20. This would indicate that the option's price move will be 20% of the price move of the underlying. Now let's suppose our underlying stock moves up from ₹100 to ₹102. This is a 2-point move. With a Delta of 0.20, our option's premium will now change by 20% of ₹2 i.e., ₹0.40, and the option's price will therefore become ₹1.0 + 0.40 = ₹1.40.

Delta Also Indicates the Probability of an Option Expiring In-the-Money (ITM)

In the case of our example above, 0.20 Delta tells us that there are 20% chances of that option becoming ITM at the time of expiry. If the option has a Delta of 0.30, it would suggest that there is a 30% chance of the option finishing in-the-money at expiry. So, basically, the absolute value of an option's Delta gives us the approximate probability of it option finishing in-the-money at expiry.

Please keep in mind that traders usually refer to the delta in absolute form. For example, a 0.25 delta is usually referred to as 25 delta, and so on.

Other Key Points to Remember about Delta

- If an option's Delta is less than 50, the option is said to be out-of-the-money (OTM).
- If an option's Delta is greater than 50, the option is said to be in-the-money (ITM).
- If an option's Delta is equal to, or close to, 50 the option is said to be at-the-money (ATM).

Concept of Neutral Delta

As we noted above, calls have a positive delta while puts have a negative delta. Accordingly:

- Being long on a call, i.e. buying a call, will result in a positive Delta. Conversely, being short on a call, i.e. selling a call, results in a negative Delta.

- Being long on a put, i.e. buying a put results in negative Delta. Conversely, being short on a put, i.e. selling a put, results in positive Delta.

Let's say we sell 5 call options of 40 Delta. We then have a Delta position of –40 × 5 = –200.

In order to be Delta neutral, we must then either:

- Sell put options having cumulative Delta of +200; or
- Buy call options of the next expiry, having a cumulative Delta of +200.

By doing so the position becomes zero Delta, or Delta neutral. **Delta neutral trading is the construction of such trades that do not react to small changes in the spot price of the underlying stock or index.** Whether the price of the underlying goes up or down, a delta neutral trade position maintains its value and neither increases nor falls in price.

We will use the Delta neutral concept to construct hedged strategies for options trading, which will be described later in the book. You would recollect that hedged trading strategies enable an option trader to sell, or write, options by depositing relatively lower margins, compared to selling naked options.

For example, let's suppose ITC is trading at around ₹250 and the Delta of 220PE and 290CE is close to –0.10 and

0.10, respectively. Remember, PE has negative Delta while CE has positive Delta. In order to create a Delta neutral position, one would to sell both the legs, involving a margin of ₹1.25 lakhs. If you decide to sell only one of the legs, you would need to keep around ₹1 lakh in your trading account as margin money. So, you see, making Delta neutral position not only secures your position but the margin money required is also lower in comparison to selling the two different option legs separately. The latter trade would also not be a Delta neutral position.

How to Select Strikes Using Delta

Since the value of Delta changes with a change in the underlying's spot price, Delta also helps us to evaluate the likely change in the option's price. Clearly, this is very useful information for options traders. Here is how.

Suppose a large IT company is going to announce its annual result during market hours. You believe that this would lead to the stock's price going up by, say, 100 points by market closing. Based on such an assumption, you would want to buy the stock's options. Some of the few choices you might have are listed below:

- Call Option-1 having a Delta of 0.30;
- Call Option-2 having a Delta of 0.80; and
- Call Option-3 having a Delta of 0.01.

Which of the three options you choose would obviously depend on which of the above three listed options will give you the maximum profits. So, let's calculate the various profit scenarios.

Change in the underlying stock's price = ₹100
Change in Call Option-1's premium = 0.30 × ₹100 = ₹30
Change in Call Option-2's premium = 0.80 × ₹100 = ₹80
Change in Call Option-3's premium = 0.01 × ₹100 = ₹1.

So, you might want to go with Call Option-2 because that would give you the biggest profit.

We can do a similar calculation in the case of put options as well.

Suppose there is a border conflict going on and you feel that it might well take a turn for the worse in the coming days. You choose a public sector bank to trade and you think that it will fall by 100 points by the expiry day. Below are a few of the put options that you might have to pick from:

- Put Option-1 having Delta of –0.30;
- Put Option-2 having Delta of –0.80; and
- Put Option-3 having Delta of –0.01.

Which of the three options you choose would again depend upon which of them would give you the maximum profit. Let's calculate the various profit scenarios.

Change in the underlying stock's price = ₹–100
Change in Put Option-1's premium = –0.30 × ₹–100 = ₹30
Change in Put Option-2's premium = –0.80 × ₹–100 = ₹80
Change in Put Option-3's premium = –0.01 × ₹–100 = ₹1.

So, again, you might want to go with the Put Option-2 because that would give you the maximum profit.

The above example highlights one more aspect which we discussed at the very beginning of our discussion on Delta. The closer the Delta is to 1, the more closely the option's price will track the underlying's stock price. Call Option-2 has a Delta of 0.80 and hence for a 100-point up move in the underlying, the option's price will rise by 80 points. Similarly, Put Option-2 has Delta of –0.80 and hence for a 100-point move downward in the underlying, the option's price will fall by 80 points.

~

Now, we need to examine what happens to Delta when the underlying's price changes. The answer is that Delta itself also changes with the underlying's price movement. This rate of change of Delta is measured by another Greek, named Gamma.

Gamma

Gamma tells us the rate at which Delta would change as the underlying's price changes.

To understand this better, let's assume you are driving a car at 50 kilometers per hour (kmph). If you increase your car's speed to 60 kmph, you would have accelerated by 10 kmph. Now, if you were to think of the car's speed as Delta, then the change in its speed is Gamma. In other words, Gamma is akin to acceleration.

In our previous discussion on Delta, we have seen that Delta measures changes in an option's price. Now let's try to understand how an option's Delta will change because of Gamma.

In our previous example of a large IT company about to announce its annual results, we had taken a view that its stock price would go up before the end of the trading session. Of course, if the result in not as per this expectation, the stock price could actually fall as well.

Let's say the current price of the stock is ₹500 and we have chosen a strike of 550 call option which has a Delta 0.40 and Gamma of 0.02*.

---

* The values of Delta and Gamma for a stock or index can be found in any of the online resources which are listed in the last section of this chapter.

Let's now understand the effect of Gamma in changing the value of Delta which, in turn, ultimately results in a change in the option's premium.

> Current price of the underlying stock = ₹500
> Delta of the chosen strike = 0.40
> Gamma of the chosen strike = 0.02

If the stock price goes up to ₹501, the new Delta of the chosen strike would be Delta plus Gamma, i.e. 0.40 + 0.02 = 0.42.

Remember, Delta tells us by how many points the option premium would change for every 1-point change in the underlying's price. After a 1-point change in the underlying's price, the new value of Delta itself is derived from Gamma which is nothing but the rate of change of Delta for every 1-point change in the underlying's price. So, in this case Delta has changed from 0.40 to 0.42 as described above.

On the other hand, if the stock price were to go down to ₹499, the new Delta of the chosen strike will be: 0.40 – 0.02 = 0.38.

We can also do a similar calculation in the case of put options.

Calculating Gamma

It's useful to also understand how Gamma is calculated. Gamma is the difference between the two values of Delta, divided by the change in the underlying's price.

> Gamma = (Delta 1 – Delta 2) ÷ (Underlying's price 1 – Underlying's price 2)

As per our previous example:

> Delta is 42 when stock price is ₹501
> Delta is 38 when stock price is ₹499
> Gamma = (42 – 38) ÷ (501 – 499)
> = 4 ÷ 2
> = 2

So, Gamma is basically the rate of change in Delta for a 1-point change in the underlying's price.

Further, just like Delta, Gamma is also dynamic.

- Gamma starts to increase when the underlying's price starts approaching the option's strike price.
- ATM strikes have the highest Gamma. That's because the Delta of the ATM strike is most sensitive to the underlying's price movement.

- On the other hand, Gamma reduces in the case of ITM and OTM strikes.

Theta

Theta measures the decay of the option premium due to the passage of time. Simply stated, Theta tells us how much the premium will reduce with each passing day till the option's expiry. For this reason, Theta is always negative. In the previous chapter we learnt that an option's premium is made up of two components, namely:

1. Intrinsic value, and
2. Extrinsic value, or time value.

Time value an option is the portion of premium in excess of its intrinsic value before expiration. The longer the time available before expiry, the greater is the option's time value.

Time value = Option premium – Intrinsic value

In order to work out the time value of an option, whether a call option or a put option, you need to calculate its intrinsic value, and subtract that from the option's premium. Whatever is left will be the time value.

The loss in the time value of an option premium is called Theta decay. Greater the time to expiry, greater would be the time value — and hence greater the value of Theta.

Suppose the option premium for our chosen strike is ₹4, and Theta is (–) 0.20. This tells us that with each passing day, the option premium will fall by ₹0.20. At the end of the first day, the option premium will be ₹3.80, and so on. The Theta decay may be greater on a Friday because the trader will lose two more days over the weekend though there is no option trading during the weekend. Thus, as time passes, the chances of the option becoming in-the-money reduce.

Think for a minute here. If this option Greek tells us about decay in premium, who will benefit from this? Clearly, option sellers will. Remember, Theta decay works in favor of option sellers and works against option buyers.

In fact, Delta and Theta are the most important Greeks for option sellers.

Weekly Expiry and Theta

SEBI has also introduced weekly expiries for Nifty and Bank Nifty derivatives. Weekly expiries happen on Thursdays. For individual stocks there is no change, and they continue to expire on the last Thursday of the month. So, if you are a stock options trader, there will be no change. But if you trade in Nifty or Bank Nifty options, it will make a difference for you.

For weekly expiries, Theta or time decay will be greater in comparison to monthly expiries because weekly options expire in 7 days while monthly options have 30 days to expire. We know that longer the time available before expiry, the greater is the option's time value. However, option premiums will also be lower for weekly expiries because of lower time values.

Vega

This Greek is related to implied volatility (IV) and tells us how much the option premium would change for each percentage change in the underlying's implied volatility.

As a rule, higher the volatility of the underlying, the more expensive the options contract is. In high volatility conditions option sellers will benefit because option premiums will be high, and so they will collect higher premium. If volatility thereafter comes down, premiums will also come down and the option seller will nevertheless get keep the profits.

On the other hand if volatility is low, options will trade at lower premiums. If an options trader buys an option at this point and subsequently if volatility goes up, premiums will also go up and the option buyer will be benefited.

Here we need to clearly understand what implied volatility is. You can obtain an option's IV from the relevant Option Chain (OI), explained in Chapter 3.

If IV is 10% for a particular option strike, whether a call or a put option, it means that the market expects the option's premium of that particular strike to move 10%, in either the positive or the negative direction, from now till the option's expiry day. Let's assume that the option premium of this strike is ₹4 and its Vega is 0.11.

Let's further assume that there is some positive news about the underlying stock, say about some business expansion plans of the company, due to which the volatility for this strike increases by 1% and becomes 11%. Correspondingly, our new option premium will be ₹4 + 0.11 = ₹4.11, because Vega for our option strike is 0.11.

On the other hand, if there is some negative news about the underlying stock, say, news of lower production or lower profit, the volatility for the strike would still increase by 1% and become 11%. As a result, our new option premium will be ₹4 – 0.11 = ₹3.89, because Vega for our option strike is 0.11.

So, volatility is not about the direction of the move. Vega is what increases or reduces the option's premium on the basis of volatility.

Vega is, thus, directly related to implied volatility.

Now, what causes implied volatility to change? Well, there can be multiple reasons, such as positive or negative news related to the underlying stock, earnings or bonus announcement for a giant organization, industry events like merger or split up of companies, or changing perceptions about the overall economy.

The market witnesses higher volatility when it is more uncertain about the future, and *vice versa*.

So:

- Greater the volatility, more unstable is the market, and higher will be the option premiums.
- Lower the volatility, more stable is the market, and hence lower will be the option premiums.

Vega is always the highest for ATM strikes, and reduces if we go to ITM or OTM strikes.

The value of Vega also depends on the time remaining for the option's expiry. Thus, for the same strike price, Vega of the next month's expiry will always be more than that for the current month's expiry. For example, if we have a 12,000PE option expiring in September and another 12,000PE option expiring in the month of October, the latter option will have a greater Vega. This is so because with a longer time remaining to expiry, the October options will have greater volatility, and hence a higher Vega. Accordingly, as an option approaches expiration and loses time value, its Vega also goes down.

How to Determine an Option's Premium Using Greeks

So far we have calculated option premiums individually for each Greek. Now, let's understand how to calculate the option premium combining together all the Greeks. This will further strengthen our understanding of option Greeks, and their effect on an option's premium.

Let's assume we have a stock priced at ₹480, and its 500CE option has the following values:

Option premium = ₹13
Delta = 40
Gamma = 0.50
Theta = 0.20
Vega = 0.10
Volatility = 12%

If the underlying stock's prices rise from its current level of ₹480 to ₹500 in the next 15 days, and volatility drops to 11%, what would be the option's premium? Let's calculate all the Greeks one by one.

First, we will calculate the change in Delta.

As we've learnt, the change in Delta is measured using Gamma.

Change in Delta = Gamma × Price movement (₹500 - ₹480).
= 0.50 × 20
= 10

So, the change in Delta is 10, and our new Delta will be: 40 + 10 = 50.

To calculate the time decay, or Theta, we will check how much time there is left for its expiry.

Theta = Theta × Number of days to expiry
= 0.20 × 15
= 3.

Please remember that Theta decay is always negative. So in this come, that will be –3.

Vega is calculated by multiplying Vega value with the change in percentage of IV.

New Vega = 0.10 × –1 (since volatility has dropped from 12% to 11%)
= –0.10

We have taken –1 for volatility change because volatility is dropping in this example. If volatility were increase to from 12% to, let's say, 14%, our new Vega will be in the positive and hence it will increase the new premium. Remember, while discussing Vega we saw that the option premium increases with an increase in volatility. This is just a working example of that concept. For now, let's stick to 11% volatility which has dropped from 12%.

With this, we have all the components to calculate the new option premium. Let's see how.

New option premium = Old option premium + Change in Delta + Theta decay + Vega
= 13 + 10 + (–3) + (–0.10)
= 19.9.

So, our new option premium will be ₹19.90.

I would suggest that you go through the above example multiple times. Try to think of hypothetical scenarios, and try to calculate the new premiums using different values.

Option Greeks in a Nut Shell

Table 3.1 summarizes all the Greeks that we have discussed till now, along with their definitions and the effect of each on an option's premium.

Table 3.1

Option Greeks in a Nut Shell

Greek	*Definition*	*Effect on Option Premium*
Delta	Change in option premium for every one point change in the price of the underlying stock or index.	▪ Delta is positive for long call options as well as for short put options. ▪ Delta is negative for short call options and for long put options.
Gamma	Change in an option's Delta.	Gamma is always positive for both calls and puts.
Theta	Rate of change of the option premium due to the passage of time or the decay.	Theta is negative for both call and put options.
Vega	Change in the option premium for each percentage change in the option's implied volatility (IV).	Vega is always positive for both call and put options.

Additional Resources

In this chapter we have discussed the various option Greeks and how to understand or interpret them for a clearer picture of the risks inherent in trading an option. I am providing two online resources from where you can get value of the option Greeks for a certain strike price.

- https://opstra.definedge.com/
- https://web.sensibull.com/

You can register yourself with your email ID and can view and analyze various option Greeks on these websites. The above websites have both free and premium subscriptions. Option chains with Greeks are available for free accounts as well.

Summary

In this chapter we saw what option Greeks are — and their impact on option prices.

From an option selling perspective, the perspective that we are focused on in this book, the most important Greeks are Delta and Theta.

Some online resources are also provided in the book which will help you to analyze which trading setup would work best for you.

With a basic knowledge of Greeks, we are now almost ready to get to grips with various option trading strategies. But, before that, we need to understand how we can form a view about the market's future, which is explained in Chapter 4.

4

~

Where is the Market Headed?

"Greed, fear and panic is the most dangerous trinity working against traders."

This chapter talks about how you can form a view or perspective about the market's near-term future. This is an important step in your trading journey.

To succeed at it, you need to be very clear about what you want to achieve from trading the market. Remember, the market is limitless, both in terms of profit — or loss. You need to decide your limits, be it with respect to profit or loss, and set clear guidelines for yourself about exiting from your trades once your objectives are met, or if your trade runs into trouble.

Clearly, no book in the world can teach anyone self-control; this you need to learn, practice, and master on your own. As has been mentioned earlier in the book, without hedging, options can be a very dangerous instrument to trade. One wrong trade and your entire capital could evaporate. But if you have a proper stop-loss, or any other defined risk measure in place, you will be saved from big losses most of the time.

Market View

To succeed in options trading, you need to have a clear view about where you believe the market is headed, particularly till the relevant expiry. Typically, this is not such a difficult thing to do. If you closely watch the market for a few weeks, you will start to get a feel of its movement. You might even be freely predicting what may be the direction of the market in the coming days, based on some event like the upcoming Union Budget, or some news of a border conflict. You may also predict that the market might be range-bound for a couple of days as there is no significant news, or because there is both positive and negative news floating around. For example, if government is about to launch a reform policy which may benefit the market directly or indirectly, and if in the same week there is also some negative news like regressive fiscal growth predictions for next quarter, then you may reasonably expect the market to be range bound since effects of both positive and negative news will tend to cancel each other.

A visual assessment of the market's chart over a period of time is another one way. But if you have to bet your money on it, I would suggest that you should learn and understand some important technical indicators of the stock market. Data on these indicators are widely available, and for free, on many trading platforms. If you enter a trade using these indicators, not only will you know when to enter a trade, but you will also get pointers as to when you should either exit the trade, or make an adjustment in the ongoing trade.

Let us consider these technical indicators one by one.

Put to Call Ratio (PCR)

This is a very important technical indicator which can help you understand the overall market sentiment surrounding a stock or an index. Using this indicator a trader can gauge where the market could head in the forthcoming days — and trade accordingly.

Calculating the PCR Value

In order to calculate PCR value, you need to see the option chain of a derivative instrument. To get the option chain, go to https://www.nseindia.com/ in your web browser and search for 'NIFTY'. Then go to the derivative tab and there you will see the 'Expiry Date' dropdown. Select any date, and you should see an options chain like the one shown in Table 4.1.

Table 4.1

~

Calculating PCR using an Options Chain

					CALLS										PUTS					
OI	CHNG IN OI	Volume	IV	**LTP**	CHNG	BID Qty	BID Price	ASK Price	ASK Qty	**STRIKE Price**	BID Qty	BID Price	ASK Price	ASK Qty	CHNG	**LTP**	IV	Volume	CHNG IN OI	OI
522	131	311	28.49	**441.75**	-123.55	675	411.20	416.10	75	**11,100**	1,725	14.65	14.80	1,350	6.10	**14.75**	30.45	74,883	-1,650	10,940
149	115	235	32.86	**365.00**	-162.75	600	365.00	365.50	375	**11,150**	300	17.40	17.55	1,275	7.45	**17.40**	29.20	21,305	120	3,005
850	-29	584	32.63	**317.00**	-152.50	375	319.50	321.80	150	**11,200**	750	21.45	21.60	75	9.90	**21.50**	37.94	1,51,587	1,098	18,445
92	56	139	30.56	**275.00**	-148.40	75	276.55	278.95	75	**11,250**	150	27.35	27.50	600	13.85	**27.45**	26.84	38.823	-35	5,939
1,908	-522	3,119	29.10	**234.25**	-141.35	75	234.55	236.40	150	**11,300**	375	36.40	36.60	150	20.10	**36.50**	26.17	2,34,165	748	22,536
264	-2	465	26.63	**195.05**	-133.55	75	195.15	197.00	375	**11,350**	150	47.15	47.45	150	27.60	**47.40**	25.33	89,422	-1,363	6,451
3,754	-103	7,160	27.23	**159.60**	-123.15	75	159.05	159.90	75	**11,400**	450	61.25	61.65	600	36.75	**61.50**	24.55	2,95,117	-851	23,926
1,864	93	2,198	26.54	**128.40**	-111.35	75	128.20	128.95	75	**11,450**	225	78.90	79.30	150	47.95	**78.65**	23.80	1,15,585	-470	7,677
18,390	4,363	52,770	25.54	**99.65**	-98.10	75	99.35	99.70	1,650	**11,500**	75	100.60	101.00	600	61.25	**100.35**	23.16	4,52,957	-2,479	34,286
5,436	3,499	39,974	24.87	**76.20**	-82.30	150	76.00	76.20	75	**11,550**	150	126.50	127.00	75	77.70	**127.00**	22.50	1,80,632	2,711	10,594
31,314	13,816	2,26,286	24.47	**57.80**	-64.40	225	57.60	57.80	75	**11,600**	150	158.00	158.65	75	94.60	**157.80**	22.01	4,55,108	-6,637	28,407
12,018	3,939	1,17,937	24.07	**42.35**	-48.70	75	42.20	42.40	600	**11,650**	75	191.20	192.35	225	110.60	**192.35**	21.30	1,52,209	-2,954	3,771
33,066	11,511	3,73,239	23.89	**30.65**	-33.80	225	30.55	30.70	450	**11,700**	75	231.40	232.00	75	125.70	**230.85**	20.82	3,09,234	1,941	10,185
15,934	3,907	2,05,135	23.88	**22.40**	-20.65	225	22.25	22.40	1,800	**11,750**	300	270.75	272.05	75	137.40	**271.45**	19.97	99,558	1,129	2,052
42,143	18,274	4,95,617	23.89	**15.80**	-11.40	450	15.80	15.90	225	**11,800**	75	316.95	318.25	75	150.00	**316.30**	19.82	1,23,949	1,873	4,099
14,707	3,133	1,82,362	24.10	**11.35**	-4.85	75	11.30	11.40	1,875	**11,850**	75	360.90	362.75	75	154.25	**360.50**	19.56	13,306	137	472
32,827	11,198	3,72,215	24.56	**8.50**	-1.25	8,550	8.40	8.45	1,875	**11,900**	75	409.45	410.50	150	159.65	**409.85**	-	22,857	510	1,085
9,950	1,191	1,23,271	25.12	**6.20**	0.05	1,200	6.15	6.25	2,100	**11,950**	150	455.85	461.15	75	161.45	**459.40**	34.23	476	84	150
43,069	9,895	3,17,814	26.16	**4.95**	0.50	1,800	4.95	5.00	16,200	**12,000**	225	504.45	507.10	75	161.80	**504.55**	-	5,364	231	1,122

Calculating the PCR value is very simple. On the extreme left and right, respectively, of the option chain you will see the open interest (OI) values. You just add all the OI of puts and all the OI of calls, and then you simply divide the number of puts by the number of calls and multiply the result by 100

Table 4.1 is an option chain of Nifty. Suppose the sum of the OIs of all the puts is X, and that of all the calls is Y, then PCR will be: PCR = (X/Y) × 100.

If we want to calculate the PCR value from Table 4.1, it would be:

Sum of OI of all Puts = 1,90,142

Sum of OI of all Calls = 2,68,257

PCR = (1,90,142 / 2,68,257) x 100 = 71

You can do similar calculations for any individual stock as well.

Now, let us see how we can use PCR value to our trading advantage.

- PCR > 130: Such a value would generally indicate that the market is overbought, and may decline from its current levels.
- PCR < 60: Such a value would usually indicate that market is oversold, and consequently may shoot-up from its current levels.

- PCR ~ 90: Such a value indicates that the market is slightly bullish, and may go up a bit from its current levels.
- PCR = 100: Such a value usually indicates that the market is neutral and it could go either up or down from current levels.

Now suppose on a trading day you find the PCR of SBI to be 120. Based on the above criteria, such a value would suggest that the stock is approaching the overbought zone and, consequently, may decline from there.

Max Pain

There are two types of options traders — option buyers and option sellers. Max pain theory holds that option sellers are mostly big institutions, such as investment banks, mortgage companies, etc., since such big institutions have big money to play with. Also, since their stakes are huge, they can manipulate the market's direction in order to favor their open trade positions.

This theory also holds that among option buyers, the maximum number lose money on the day of expiry. Hence, near to the expiry, the market moves in the direction of maximum losses for option buyers and, conversely, in the direction of maximum profits for option sellers.

Suppose Nifty is at 11,500, and Max pain for Nifty's current month expiry is 11,800, then the Max pain theory suggests that at 11,800 there would be maximum losses for option buyers, and in-turn maximum profits for option sellers, and the market may close near 11,800 on expiry day.

While we can calculate max pain in Microsoft Excel, but I would suggest you look for the current max pain value in websites, such as https://opstra.definedge.com/. Max pain value can give us an idea, which will not always be completely accurate, of the level the market may get to once we enter the expiry week. We can then craft our trades based on this value.

Bollinger Bands

Bollinger Bands is a technical indicator, based on the concept of standard deviation, which indicates how the market may move in the forthcoming trading sessions.

Bollinger Bands is a momentum indicator plotted using simple moving average (SMA) with the SMA's standard deviation forming its upper and lower boundaries. The chart of the Bollinger Bands in Figure 4.1 is plotted on the daily chart of Nifty. If you observe closely, from mid-June 2020 to mid-September 2020, Nifty never crossed the median line of the Bollinger Bands chart in Figure 4.1. We can use this technical indicator to predict the levels from where the market may reverse. As per the graph in Figure 4.1, there was a sharp fall in the last week of September. Had a full

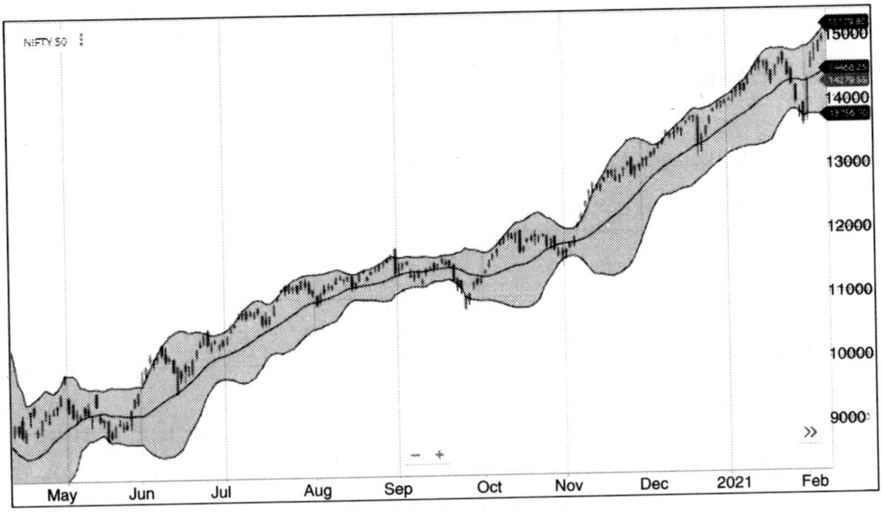

Figure 4.1: Bollinger Bands

dark candle formed below the lower boundary of the Bollinger Band, the market might then have moved down. But that didn't happen and the market didn't touch its median line until the last week of December.

The following are the general rules for interpreting Bollinger Bands:

- If the daily chart candle breaches the upper boundary of the Bollinger Bands, it suggests that the market is overbought and may reverse to its mean position, as shown in the graph of Nifty's in Figure 4.1.
- On the other hand, if a daily candle breaches the lower boundary of the Bollinger Bands, it would suggest that

the market is oversold and may reverse to its mean position.

The Bollinger Bands indicator is one of option seller's best friends as it provides an indication of the upcoming market momentum.

India VIX

India VIX, or India volatility index, is based on the Nifty index. From the best bid-ask prices of Nifty options contracts, a volatility figure, in percentage basis, is calculated which indicates the expected market volatility over the next 30 calendar days. The higher this percentage is, the greater will be the market volatility. India VIX is an indicator which moves up and down just like Nifty does, but it can't be traded on the exchange. It's generally applicable on Nifty index while individual stocks may not follow this.

Typically, the value of India VIX hovers around 15, and it starts to rise if the volatility increases. Figure 4.2 is the weekly chart of India VIX. As you can see, there was a spike in this chart around April 2020, during the first Covid-19 lockdown, when it reached 70. India VIX is inversely proportional to the Nifty Index. Thus, an increase in the India VIX represents a rise in volatility and the fall of Nifty Index. Conversely, a fall in India VIX represents a reduction in volatility and a steady increase in Nifty Index.

~

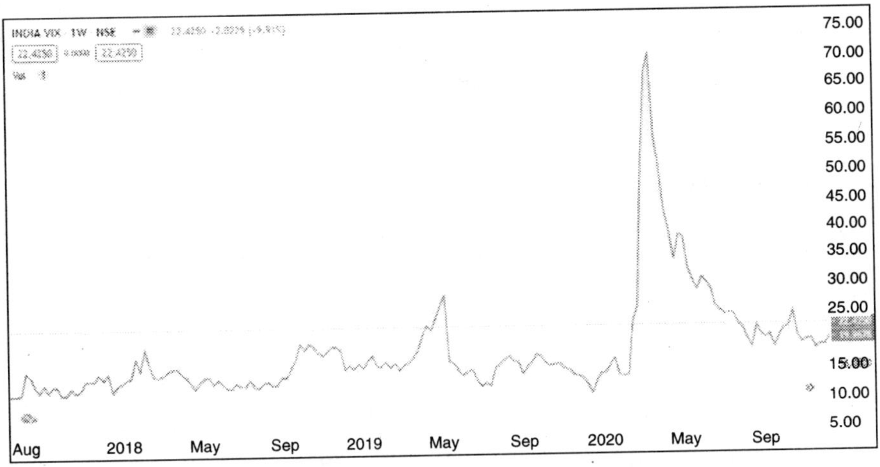

Figure 4.2: India VIX during Covid-19 in 2020

~

If you want to read more about India VIX, please check the white paper published by National Stock Exchange of India on link below.

https://www1.nseindia.com/content/indices/white_paper_IndiaVIX.pdf

~

Having a view about the market is the first step in trading. Of course, your view may not always turn out to be correct every time, or even most of the time. In case your view proves incorrect, you can make necessary adjustments during the life of the trade, as we will learn later. So, it doesn't really matter so much as an option seller if your market view is right or wrong. Actually, the real value of having a market view is that it helps you choose an appropriate options trading strategy. In case the trade later starts to go against you, you can make suitable adjustments.

Summary

In this chapter we saw how statistics suggest that selling options is more profitable than options buying. There will be times when you feel tempted to buy calls for quick profits. Instead of doing that, however, you should consider selling puts in line with your market view, and buying farther distant puts to safeguard yourself. We will discuss all these aspects in the next chapters. Apart from this, we have also covered in this chapter a few more additional concepts which would be useful when we chalk out our plan to build and manage our trade positions. Of all the mentioned topics, I would stress more on PCR and Max Pain. You can obtain their values from online resources.

5

~

Naked Trading Strategies for Option Sellers

In this chapter we will review some widely used naked option trading strategies from the option seller's perspective.

Naked option strategies can be either one-leg or two-leg strategies, but the one common feature of naked strategies is that they carry potentially unlimited risk for option sellers if the trade goes against them. Such risk can be fatal for a trading career; which is why I strongly recommend that you must never trade naked options. However, you need to understand naked option strategies in order to comprehend our preferred hedged option trading strategies, which we will tackle in the next chapter.

Let us first understand what is meant by naked options trading. When we write, namely sell, an option, whether a call option (CE) or a put option (PE), without buying any offsetting CE or PE options, respectively, it is called naked option trading. If the trade goes against the trader, a naked option setup can incur huge losses. Selling of naked options has limited rewards — the maximum profit being limited to the premium received — but unlimited loss potential.

Before we get into more details of naked strategies, however, let's first fully understand the concept of margin money.

Understanding Margin Money

Buying options is easy. You just pay the necessary premium, and that's it. No further capital or payment is required thereafter. If the underlying asset moves in your anticipated direction, the options premium increases (please re-read Chapter 3 on Options Greeks, if you need to), and you end up making money. In case the underlying security moves in the opposite direction to what you had anticipated when initiating the trade, the option's premium would fall and you would lose money.

On the other hand, when a trader sells, namely writes, options, s/he collect the premium at the start of the trade. In turn, the concerned exchange requires the option seller to deposit a certain amount with his / her broker as security in order to safeguard the option buyer's interest should the trade go against the option seller. The amount the option sellers need to deposit with their brokers is called Total Margin, or, simply, Margin. This amount will be blocked with your broker until the trade is completed and all positions are squared-off. If required, the margin money is used to square off the positions.

Total margin is made up of two components:

1. Initial margin; and
2. Exposure margin.

At NSE, the initial margin calculation is carried out using a software called SPAN (standard portfolio analysis of risk). The SPAN margin is the base margin that is calculated based on the value at risk (VAR) method. VAR takes into account the maximum loss that the particular stock can incur in a single day based on historical probabilities. SPAN uses a scenario-based approach to arrive at margins. The value of an option position depends on the price and volatility of the concerned security in the cash market. As both price and volatility keep changing, SPAN generates about 16 different scenarios by assuming various values of price and volatility. For each of these scenarios, the possible loss that a particular option position would suffer is calculated. The initial margin required to be paid by the trader would be equal to the highest loss the particular option position could suffer from among all the scenarios considered. The margin is monitored and collected at the time of placing the buy / sell order. SPAN margins are revised six times every day — once at the beginning of the day, four times during market hours, and, finally, once at the end of the day. Since initial margins are calculated using the SPAN tool, the initial margin is also called SPAN margin.

Exposure margins may be required over and above the initial margins in order to cover mark-to-market (MTM) losses. MTM or mark-to-market is the daily profit / loss, which is calculated on a day-to-day basis. To understand this better, let's assume you are long in a stock having sold an OTM put option. This means you believe that the stock's price will go up.

Now if the stock price moves up on a particular day, the put option you have sold will lose some of its premium. As a result, on that day your MTM will be positive.

Conversely, if the stock price moves down, the premium will increase and your MTM will be negative.

Let's assume that your stock's current market price is ₹100, and its derivative lot size is 4,000. You believe that the price will go up and hence you sell 90PE at a ₹3 premium. In this case the sample calculation of daily MTM would be as follows:

Day 1

The stock price moves up to ₹105 and the premium of 90PE becomes ₹2.35.

MTM = (3.0 – 2.35) × 4,000 = ₹2,600.

Day 2

The stock price moves down to ₹95 and the 90PE premium rises to ₹3.40.

MTM = (3.0 – 3.4) × 4,000 = – ₹1,600.

Day 3

The stock price moves further down to ₹90 and the 90PE premium rises to ₹4.50.

MTM = (3.0 – 4.5) × 4,000 = – ₹6,000.

Day 4

The stock rises to ₹110 and the 90PE price becomes ₹1.80.

MTM = (3.0 – 1.8) × 4,000 = ₹4,800.

So as you can see, the option premium changes due to daily market variations. With a change in your option's premium, your MTM will also change. Exposure margins are therefore required to cover any MTM losses that may occur. Thus, if there is huge volatility on a particular trading day and the market crashes, exposure margin will cover any MTM losses incurred.

Popular and Important Naked Options Strategies

To keep things simple, we will cover the following naked options trading strategies in this chapter:

- Naked selling of call options – a one-leg strategy;

- Naked selling of put options – a one-leg strategy;
- Short strangle – a two-leg naked options strategy;
- Short straddle – a two-leg naked options strategy.

One may think that only four strategies are too few but, believe me, once you have spent some time in the market you would understand that these are the key strategies based on which you can form advanced / hedged strategies involving multiple legs and multiple expiries.

~

Naked Selling of Call Options (CE)

Suppose Nifty is at 11,500, and your market view is that the index will not rise higher than 11,800 during the current expiry. Accordingly, let's say you sell 11,800CE (call option). Let's assume that the premium you collect in doing so is ₹70. Taking Nifty's lot size as 75, let's see what your profit / loss scenarios will be.

- Market view: The market will not go up beyond a certain level before expiry.
- Legs involved: One.
- Premium collected: ₹70 × 75 = ₹5,250.

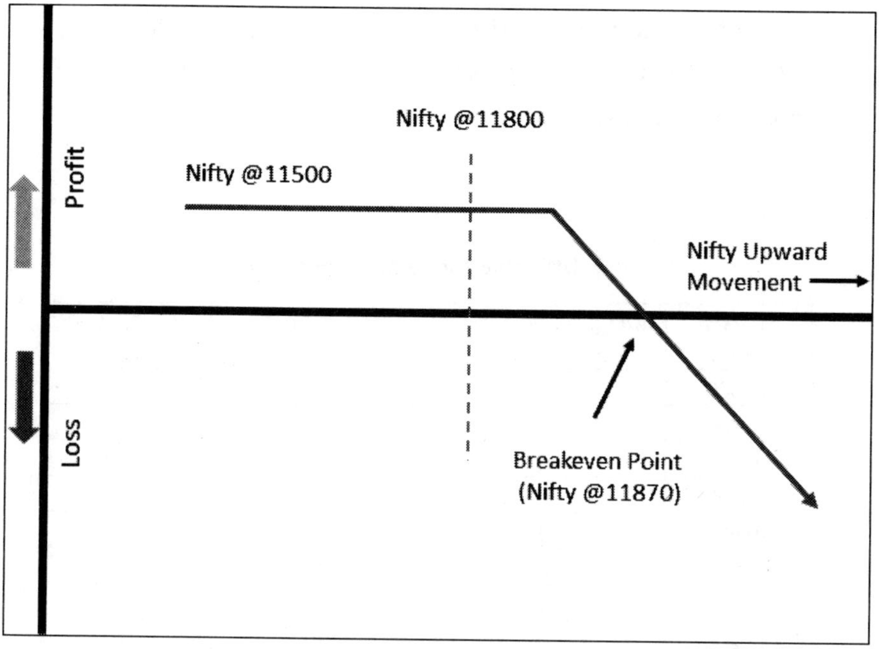

Figure 5.1: Payoff Graph for Naked Selling of Call Option (CE)

- Margin required: Around ₹90,000. Remember, naked positions require higher margins.
- Breakeven point: Strike price + premium = ₹11,800 + ₹70 = ₹11,870.
- Maximum Profit: Limited to the premium collected: ₹5,250.
- Loss: You will lose money if the market closes above 11,870 at expiry.

To understand the payoff from this strategy, let's plot a pay-off table for this trade to see how our profits will be at different market expiries.

Table 5.1

Pay-Off Table for Selling Naked Calls

Market Expiry	*MAX (0, (Market Expiry – Strike (11800)))*	*Premium Received (₹)*	*Strategy Payoff (₹)*
10,500	0	70	70
10,600	0	70	70
10,700	0	70	70
10,800	0	70	70
10,900	0	70	70
11,000	0	70	70
11,100	0	70	70
11,200	0	70	70
11,300	0	70	70
11,400	0	70	70
11,500	0	70	70
11,600	0	70	70
11,700	0	70	70
11,800	0	70	70
11,900	100	70	-30
12,000	200	70	-130
12,100	300	70	-230
12,200	400	70	-330
12,300	500	70	-430
12,400	600	70	-530
12,500	700	70	-630

The column headings of Table 5.1 are self-explanatory except for the heading of the second column – "MAX (0, (Market Expiry – Strike (11,800)))".

This column heading means:

- If the market expires at 11,600 then the outcome of this equation will be the higher of 0 and (11,600 – 11,800)
  = the higher of 0 and 200
  = 0.
- If the market expires at 12,000 then the outcome of this equation will be the higher of 0 and (12,000-11,800)
  = the higher of 0 and 200
  = 200.

As you would notice, Table 5.1 shows a constant profit of ₹70 so long as Nifty stays below 11,870, and the profit is nothing but the premium the seller collected at the outset of the trade, which is ₹70 × 75 = ₹5,250. With Nifty's lot size being 75, if Nifty stays below 11,870 the seller will be in profit, capped to the premium collected. If there is an up move and the market moves higher and closes above 11,870, you could, conceivably, suffer unlimited loss since theoretically there is no limit to how high the Nifty can go. For example, if Nifty closes at 12,000 then your loss would be ₹130 × 75 = ₹9,750.

Naked Selling of Put (PE) Option

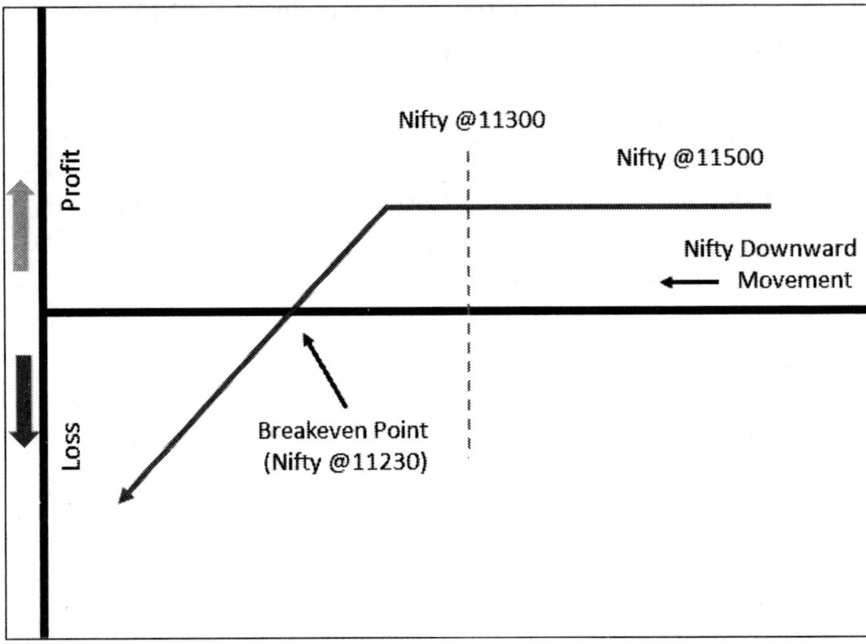

Figure 5.2: Payoff Graph for Naked Selling of a Put Option

Suppose Nifty is at 11,500, and you believe that the market is likely go somewhat higher — and even if it doesn't do so, it will not fall below 11,300 in the current expiry. As explained in Chapter 4, the statistical chances of option sellers making money are 66%, while the chances of option buyers making money are only 33%. In pursuance of higher market expectation and statistical facts, let's say you sell a put option, Nifty 11,300PE. Let's say the premium you collect is ₹70. Taking the lot size of Nifty as 75, let's see what the profit / loss scenario would be.

- Market view: The market will not fall below a certain level before expiry.
- Legs involved: One.
- Premium collected: ₹70 × 75 = ₹5,250.
- Margin required: Around ₹90,000; remember, naked sell positions require bigger margin.
- Breakeven point: Strike price – premium = ₹11,300 – 70 = ₹11,230.
- Maximum Profit: Limited to the premium collected = ₹5,250.
- Loss: You will lose money if the market closes below 11,230 on expiry date.

To understand the result from this strategy, let's plot a payoff table to see how our profits will be at different Nifty levels of market expiry.

Table 5.2

Pay-Off Table for Selling Nifty 11,300 Put

Market Expiry	*MAX (0, (Strike (11,300) - Market Expiry))*	*Premium Received*	*Strategy Payoff*
10,500	800	70	-730
10,600	700	70	-630
10,700	600	70	-530
10,800	500	70	-430
10,900	400	70	-330
11,000	300	70	-230
11,100	200	70	-130
11,200	100	70	-30
11,300	0	70	70
11,400	0	70	70
11,500	0	70	70
11,600	0	70	70
11,700	0	70	70
11,800	0	70	70
11,900	0	70	70
12,000	0	70	70
12,100	0	70	70
12,200	0	70	70
12,300	0	70	70
12,400	0	70	70
12,500	0	70	70

All the column headings of Table 5.2 are self-explanatory, except for the caption of the second column – "MAX (0, (Strike (11,300) – Market Expiry))".

This heading denotes that:

- If the market expires at 11,600 then the outcome for the trader will be:
  = MAX (0, (11,300 – 11,600)), i.e. the higher of 0 and (11,300 – 11,600)
  = MAX (0, –300), i.e. the higher of 0 and –300
  = 0.
- If the market expires at 10,700 then the outcome for the trader will be:
  = MAX (0, (11,300 – 10,700)) — i.e. the higher of 0 and (11,300 – 11,700).
  = MAX (0, 600) — i.e. the higher of 0 and 600.
  = 600.

Table 5.2 also shows a constant profit of ₹70, so long as Nifty stays above 11,230. This is nothing but the premium the seller collected at the start of the trade, which is 70 × 75 = ₹5,250, 75 being the lot size of Nifty.

So if Nifty stays above 11,230, you will be in profit, limited to the premium collected. If the market falls and the Nifty closes below 11,230, you will lose money. For example, if Nifty closes at 11,000 then your loss would be 230 × 75 = –₹17,250. As per Table 5.2, if Nifty closes at 10,500 then your loss would be ₹730 × 75 = ₹54,750, and so on.

Short Strangle

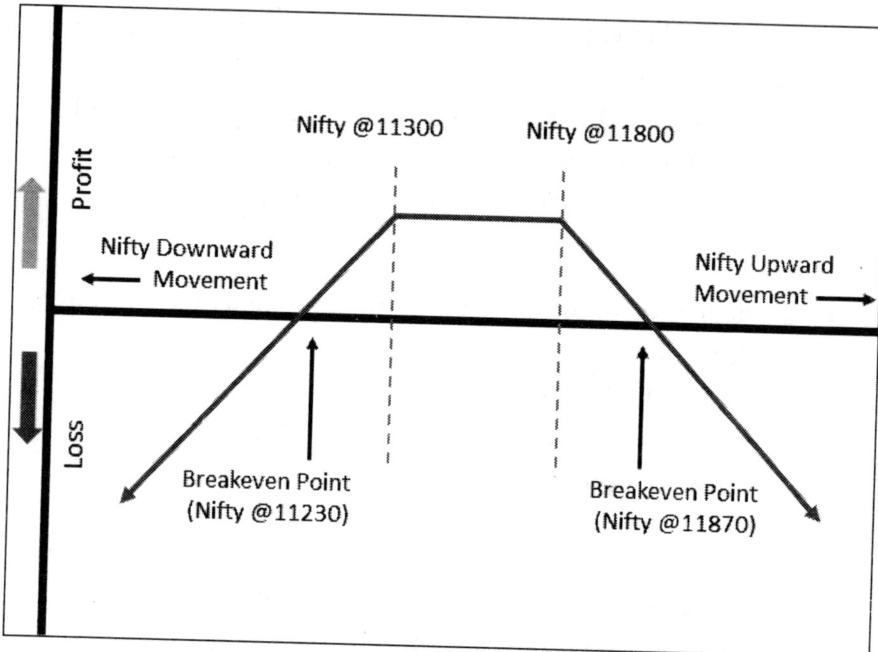

Figure 5.3: Payoff Graph for a Short Strangle

A short strangle consists of a short CE with a higher strike price, and another short PE with a lower strike. Both options have the same underlying, whether stock or index, and also the same expiration date.

A short strangle is initiated for a net credit and it yields profits so long as the underlying stock or index trades between the break-even points of its two legs. A short strangle's profit potential is limited to the total premiums received when the trade is initiated. The potential loss is unlimited if the stock price rises, or falls, beyond the respective break-even points.

Short strangle is a delta neutral strategy, i.e. overall delta of the trade is 0. You would recall that we had discussed the concept of delta neutral in Chapter 3.

Suppose Nifty is at 11,500, and you believe that it will remain ranged between 11,300 and 11,800 during the current expiry.

In this case, the negative and positive delta of 11,300PE (put option) and 11,800CE (call option), respectively, are canceling each other. Let's say you have sold both 11,300PE and 11,800CE. Let's further suppose that you have collected a premium of ₹70 for each leg. Taking the lot size of Nifty as 75, let's review the profit and loss scenario for this trade.

- Market view: The market will be range-bound till expiry. In this case the trader expects Nifty to be range bound between the band of 11,300 and 11,800.
- Legs involved: Two.
- Premium collected: ₹(70 + 70) × 75 = ₹10,500.
- Margin required: Approximately ₹1,50,000.
- Lower break even point: Strike price – premium = 11,300 – 70 = 11,230.

Table 5.3

Pay-Off Table for the Short Strangle Example

1	2	3	4	5	6
Market Expiry	*CE Outcome = Higher of 0 and Market Expiry Price minus Strike Price (11,800)*	*CE Payoff (Premium Received - CE Outcome)*	*PE Outcome = Higher of 0 and Strike Price (11,300) minus Market Expiry Price*	*PE Payoff (Premium Received - PE Outcome)*	*Strategy Payoff (CE + PE Payoff)*
10,500	0	70	800	-730	-660
10,600	0	70	700	-630	-560
10,700	0	70	600	-530	-460
10,800	0	70	500	-430	-360
10,900	0	70	400	-330	-260
11,000	0	70	300	-230	-160
11,100	0	70	200	-130	-60
11,200	0	70	100	-30	40
11,300	0	70	0	70	140
11,400	0	70	0	70	140
11,500	0	70	0	70	140
11,600	0	70	0	70	140
11,700	0	70	0	70	140
11,800	0	70	0	70	140
11,900	100	-30	0	70	40
12,000	200	-130	0	70	-60
12,100	300	-230	0	70	-160
12,200	400	-330	0	70	-260
12,300	500	-430	0	70	-360
12,400	600	-530	0	70	-460
12,500	700	-630	0	70	-560

- Upper break even point: Strike price + premium = 11,800 + 70 = 11,870.

- Maximum Profit: Limited to the premium collected = ₹10,500.
- Profit / Loss: You will lose money if the market closes either below 11,230, or above 11,870, at expiry. Otherwise, the trade will be in profit.

To understand the payoff from this strategy, let's review the pay-off table for this short strangle trade (*see* Table 5.3) to understand our profit picture at different market expiries.

The various column headings of Table 5.3 are self-explanatory, except for the headings of columns 2 and 4.

The heading of Column 2, namely new line "CE Outcome = MAX (0, (Market Expiry – Strike (11,800)))" new line refers to the following outcomes from shorting the call option. Means that the outcome will be the higher of 0, and the underlying's market expiry price, minus 11,800.

If the market were to expire at 11,600, the result of the trade would be:

The higher of 0, and (Market Expiry Price – Strike (11,800))
= the higher of 0, and (11,600 –11,800)
= the higher of 0, and –200
= 0.

The heading of Column 4, namely, new line "PE Outcome = MAX (0, (Strike (11,300) – Market Expiry))" new line refers to the outcomes from shorting the put option. The outcome would be the higher of 0 and strike price minus the price at market expiry.

If market expires at 11,000, then the result of the short put trade would be:

The higher of 0, and (Strike (11,300) – price of the underlying at market expiry)
= the higher of 0, and (11,300 – 11,000)
= the higher of 0, and 300
= 300.

Table 5.3 also reveals that the trade would be in profit so long as Nifty stays either above 11,230, or below 11,870. The maximum profit, as shown in Table 5.3, would ₹140 × 75 = ₹10,500, which is nothing but the premium collected.

In case there is a downtrend in the market and Nifty closes below 11,230, you would incur a loss. For example, if Nifty closes at 11,000 then the loss would be ₹160 × 75 = ₹12,000. On the other hand, if the market were to rise and close above, say, 11,870, you would again have a loss. For example, if the Nifty closes at 12,000 then your loss would be ₹60 × 75 = ₹4,500.

Short Straddle

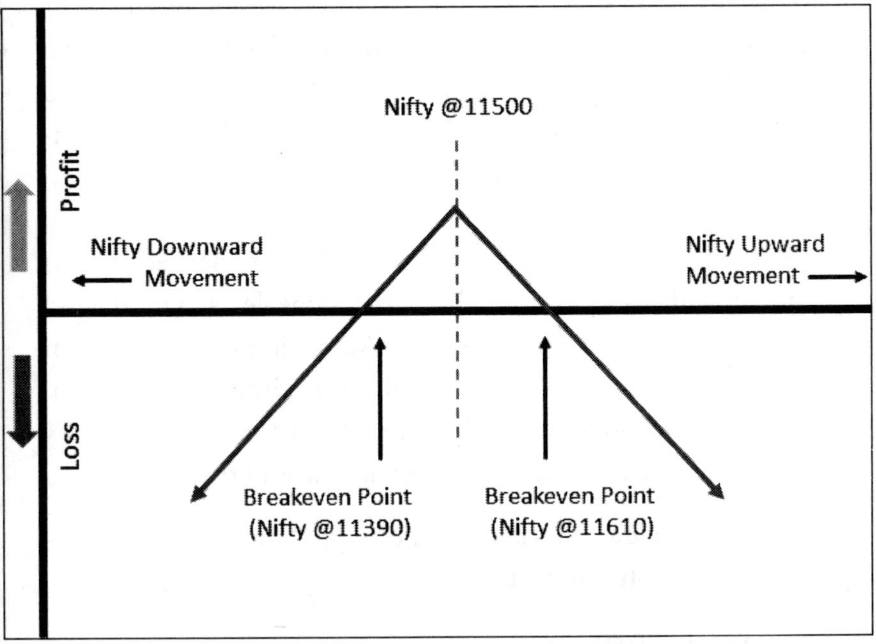

Figure 5.4: Payoff Graph for a Short Straddle

Let's now consider the short straddle, which is another delta neutral strategy. A short straddle consists of one short CE and one short PE. Both options have the same underlying stock or Index, the same strike price, and the same expiration date. Remember, the short strangle discussed earlier had two legs with different strike prices.

A short straddle is initiated for a net credit — namely the option seller receives premium as a result of selling the two options, and it would be profitable if the underlying stock or Index trades between the two break-even points. The maximum profit potential of this trade is limited to the total premium received. The potential loss, however, is unlimited if the stock price rises, or falls, beyond the respective break-even points of the two legs.

Let's suppose Nifty is at 11,500, and your market view is that it will also close at about the same level, i.e. around 11,500, in the current expiry. Accordingly, you sell an 11,500PE put option and also sell an 11,500CE call option. Let's say the premium collected is ₹110 for each leg. Let's see what your profit and loss scenario would then be.

- Market view: Market will be range bound and may expire near the current levels.
- Legs involved: Two.
- Premium collected: ₹(110 + 110) × 75 = ₹16,500.
- Margin required: Around ₹1,60,000.
- Lower breakeven point: Strike price – premium = ₹11,500 – ₹110 = ₹11,390.
- Upper breakeven point: Strike price + premium = ₹11,500 + ₹110 = ₹11,610.
- Maximum Profit: Limited to the premium collected = ₹16,500.
- Loss: You will lose money if the market either closes below 11,390, or closes above 11,610 at expiry.

To understand the payoff from this trade, let's look at Table 5.4 to understand what the profits from this trade would be at different levels of market expiry.

Table 5.4

Pay-Off Table for the Short Straddle

1	2	3	4	5	6
Market Expiry	*CE Outcome = MAX (0, (Market Expiry - Strike (11,500)))*	*CE Payoff (Premium Received - CE Outcome)*	*PE Outcome = MAX (0, (Strike (11,500) - Market Expiry))*	*PE Payoff (Premium Received - PE Outcome)*	*Strategy Payoff (CE + PE Payoff)*
10,500	0	110	1,000	-890	-780
10,600	0	110	900	-790	-680
10,700	0	110	800	-690	-580
10,800	0	110	700	-590	-480
10,900	0	110	600	-490	-380
11,000	0	110	500	-390	-280
11,100	0	110	400	-290	-180
11,200	0	110	300	-190	-80
11,300	0	110	200	-90	20
11,400	0	110	100	10	120
11,500	0	110	0	110	220
11,600	100	10	0	110	120
11,700	200	-90	0	110	20
11,800	300	-190	0	110	-80
11,900	400	-290	0	110	-180
12,000	500	-390	0	110	-280
12,100	600	-490	0	110	-380
12,200	700	-590	0	110	-480
12,300	800	-690	0	110	-580
12,400	900	-790	0	110	-680
12,500	1,000	-890	0	110	-780

Column 2 lists the outcomes arising from shorting the call option.

The heading of Column 2 reads as follows: CE Outcome = MAX (0, (Market Expiry – Strike (11,500))).

This means that the outcome of the trade would be the higher of 0 and the difference of the underlying's price at market expiry minus the strike price.

Thus, if the market expires at 11,000, then the outcome of the trade would be:

The higher of 0 and (market price at expiry– 11,500, i.e. the strike price)
= the higher of 0 and (11,000 –11,500)
= the higher of 0 and –500
= 0.

Column 4 of Table 5.4 lists the various possible outcomes of shorting (selling) the put option.

The heading of Column 4 reads as follows: PE Outcome = MAX (0, (Strike (11,500) – Market Expiry)).

This means that the outcome of this leg of the trade would be the higher of 0 and the difference between the strike price and the underlying's market price at expiry.

Thus, if the market expires at 11,200 then this leg's outcome expiry would be the higher of 0, and the difference between the strike price, i.e. 11,500, minus the market price at expiry.
= the higher of 0, and (11,500 –11,200))
= the higher of 0, and 300
= 300.

Accordingly, Table 5.4 shows that the trade will be profitable if Nifty either stays above 11,390, or below 11,610. The maximum profit, as Table 5.4 shows, will be ₹220 × 75 = ₹16,500, which is nothing but the premium you collected at the initiation of the trade.

If the market falls and the index closes below 11,390, you will lose. You will also lose if the index were to close above 11,610.

For example, if Nifty closes at 11,000 then your loss will be ₹280 × 75 = ₹21,000. If the market were to rise and close above 11,610, you will again lose. For example, if Nifty closes at 12,000 then your loss will be ₹280 × 75 = ₹21,000.

Revisiting the Greeks – Briefly

When you create either a short strangle or a short straddle, you are creating a delta neutral strategy. Once the market starts to move, the delta of the threatened side, namely the side towards which the market is moving, whether up or down, will increase much faster than the delta of the non-threatened side.

Examples

For example, let's say I want to create a short strangle. Now, let's suppose Nifty is at 11,500, and to create a short strangle I have sold an 11,300PE and an 11,800CE. Let's further suppose that along comes some negative news and Nifty falls to 11,350. In real life scenario, the delta of 11,300PE will be much larger than the delta of 11,800CE. You may ask how.

We know that delta of at-the-money (ATM) options is 50. Thus, when Nifty was at 11,500, its ATM strike must have had a delta of 50. Let's assume that Delta of 11,300PE is 30 and delta of 11,800CE is also 30. Now when Nifty gets to 11,350, its current ATM strike will be 11,350, which is very close to our sold strike, that is 11,300PE. And since the underlying's price is very close to 11,300, its delta will also be very close to 50. Thus, the delta of 11,300PE has increased from 30 to almost 50. On the other hand, 11,800CE was an out-of-the-money (OTM) option when we sold it, and which is now a far OTM. And since it's a far OTM option, its delta will be even lower, maybe around 10.

Apart from this, Vega will also be the highest for an ATM strike. So, ATM strikes with the highest Vega will be more volatile, and hence would command greater premium than would far OTM strikes. This means that you will lose more money on the 11,300PE leg than you will earn on the 11,800CE leg as Nifty moves from 11,500 to 11,350.

~

The above example was a theoretical one. Let us now try to understand such premium changes with the help of a real-life example.

State Bank of India (NSE: SBIN) was trading at ₹194.75 on 20 August 2020. The August 2020 monthly expiry was due on 27 August. Since SBIN price had been hovering at around ₹195 for quite some time, let's assume that you decided to create a short straddle. At that time, one lot of SBIN used to comprise of 3,000 shares. The trade computation would be as follows.

- Price of SBIN on 20 August 2020 = ₹194.75
- Days to expiry = 7 days (Expiry Date: 27 August 2020)
- Put option sold = 185PE at ₹1.20 premium.
- Premium collected from the put side = ₹1.20 × 3,000 = ₹3,600
- Call option sold: 205CE at ₹1.95 premium.
- Premium collected from the call side = ₹1.95 × 3,000 = ₹5,850
- Total premium collected from the short straddle = ₹3,600 + ₹5,850 = ₹9,450.

Five days later, i.e. on 25 of August 2020, SBIN was trading at ₹207.95. Since prospects of the trade were not looking good as SBIN was continuously moving higher, let's say you decided to close your positions that day. Since your positions were formed by selling options, to close them you must buy those very same options at their current market prices.

- Put option bought = 185PE at a premium of ₹0.10.
- Premium paid for buying 185PE = ₹0.10 × 3,000 = ₹300.
- Call option bought = 205CE at premium of ₹4.95
- Premium paid for buying 205CE = ₹4.95 × 3,000 = ₹14,850
- Total premium paid to close the short straddle = ₹300 + ₹14,850 = ₹15,150.
- Loss in short straddle (per lot) = Premium collected – Premium paid = ₹9,450 – ₹15,150 = ₹5,700

All these prices of the stock and option premium are actual historical prices and can be found at the following websites of NSE:

- https://www1.nseindia.com/products/content/equities/equities/eq_security.htm
- https://www1.nseindia.com/products/content/derivatives/equities/historical_fo.htm

The Vega of the threatened side increased due to greater volatility on that side and hence the rate of change of option premiums was also higher on the threatened side. Also, 205CE was an OTM strike when you took your position in the market. But as the stock price moved higher from ₹194.75, the 205CE turned ITM. Do you remember what happens to the delta of ITM options, from the chapter on Option greeks? It is always greater than 50.

Hedged strategies come into the picture precisely in order to manage these kinds of fluid and tricky situations, where the positions you have taken in the market require some protection on the threatened side.

Summary

This chapter was all about naked option strategies for option sellers. To be honest, in my initial years of trading I, too, took these kinds of risky trades both because I didn't then have a sufficient understanding of hedged strategies, and also because my trading capital was limited.

In the next chapter, we will learn about hedged strategies which are nothing but a combination of naked strategies, and which give you protection against sudden and adverse market movements.

6

~

Hedged Trading Strategies for Option Sellers

In the previous chapter we reviewed a few significant naked option trading strategies. These look simple enough to execute, but as we saw they carry the risk of higher loss — in some cases risk of unlimited loss. Hedged strategies help to mitigate such risks.

In this chapter, we will consider the most important hedged trading strategies for option sellers. Since multiple individual positions are involved in these hedged strategies, they can help limit your loss if the trade goes against your market perspective. In addition, there are several techniques to adjust hedged strategies mid-trade which can be used to minimize loss, or even to earn higher profit.

One important point to note here: hedged strategies give lower reward than naked strategies. While you do indeed collect premium, but you also pay a small premium to safeguard and insure yourself against unexpected adverse market moves. So, the trade-off is that you stand to make somewhat lower profits by using hedged strategies. On the other hand, these strategies also considerably lower your risk of loss.

We will cover the following hedged strategies in this chapter:

- Bear Call Spread – a two-leg strategy;
- Bull Put Spread – a two-leg strategy;
- Iron Condor – a four-leg strategy;
- Iron Fly – a four-leg strategy.

On the face of it, the above list may seem to comprise rather few strategies but, believe me, these are the crux of all trading strategies.

My personal favorite is the Iron Condor. This is also the strategy which most consistently successful traders use. Its application is simple and, also, there are easy ways by which you can adjust an Iron Condor in mid-trade.

Let's now discuss these strategies one by one.

Bear Call Spread

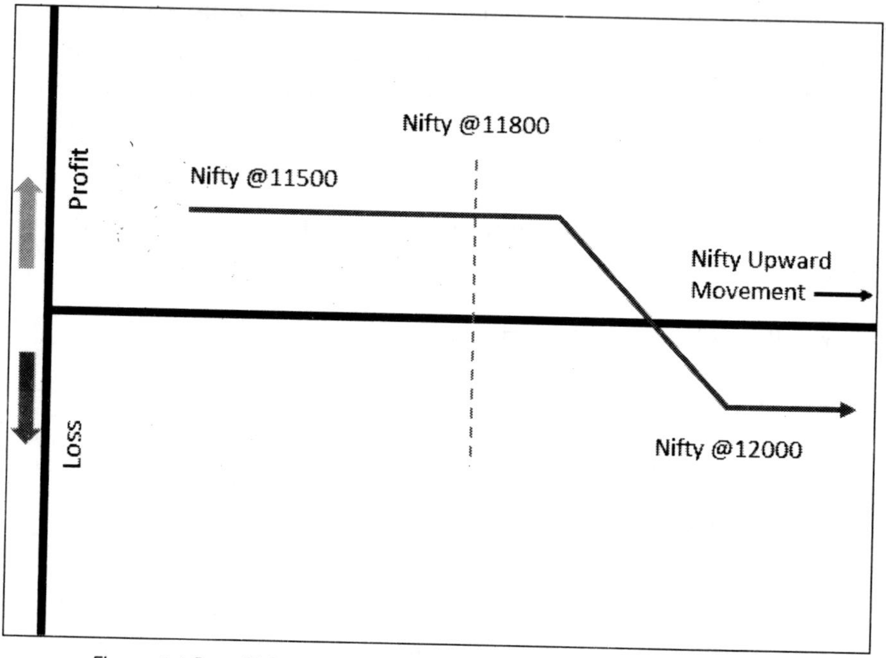

Figure 6.1: Payoff Graph for a Bear Call Spread – a two-leg strategy

As its name would suggest, you would use a bear call spread when you have a bearish view of the market.

Suppose Nifty is at 11,500, and you think that it will not rise beyond 11,800 during the current expiry. Accordingly, you sell an 11,800CE (call option) at ₹70. Remember, selling a call option has potentially unlimited risk because there is no upper limit to how high the underlying's price can rise.

To safeguard against the risk of unlimited loss, you would then also have to buy an OTM strike. Let's say you buy 12,000CE (call option) at ₹25. With the Nifty lot size of 75, let's review the profit and loss scenarios.

- Market view: Market will not go higher than a certain level before expiry.
- Legs involved: Two.
- Premium collected by selling the 11,800 call option: ₹70 × 75 = ₹5,250.
- Money spent to buy OTM 12,000 call option: ₹25 × 75 = ₹1,875
- Net premium collected = ₹5,250 – ₹1,875 = ₹3,375.
- Margin required: Around ₹60,000; remember, hedged positions require lower margin than do naked options. If you were to sell only an 11,800CE option then the margin requirement might well have been ₹100,000.

Profit / Loss Scenarios

Market Closes at Or Below 11,800

If the market closes at or below 11,800, i.e. at or below the level of your OTM sell CE strike, then the 11,800CE and 12,000CE options will expire worthless, and you will get to keep the total premium you collected, which is ₹3,375.

Market Closes above 11,800

If the market closes above 11,800 due to an unexpected up move, say it goes to 12,200, your loss will be limited to the difference between the two strike prices, minus the net premium received at the time of entering into the trade. Let's calculate this loss.

- Loss on the sell leg = (₹11,800 – ₹12,200) × 75 = ₹30,000.
- Profit on the buy leg = (₹12,200 – ₹12,000) × 75 = ₹15,000.
- Total payout (loss) = – 30,000 + 15,000 + 3,375 (premium received) = ₹11,625.

Thus, ₹11,625 would be your maximum loss if the market goes against your view. Irrespective of the level to which the market may go against you, your maximum loss in the trade will stay capped at ₹11,625, and not a rupee more. This again shows the great advantage of using hedged strategies. Had you not bought the 12,000 OTM call option, your loss on the trade would have been: –30,000 + 3,375 = ₹26,625! Further, we can lower even the loss of ₹11,625 by properly managing the trade position before expiry, as we will discuss later in Chapter 8.

Now let's review Table 6.1 to see what our profits from this strategy would be at different market expiries.

Table 6.1

Pay-Off for the (Hedged) Bear Call Spread Trade

1	2	3	4	5	6
Market Expiry	*Short Call (11,800) Outcome = MAX (0, (Market Expiry - Strike (11,800)))*	*Short Call (11,800) Payoff (Premium Received – Outcome)*	*Long Call (12,000) Outcome = MAX (0, (Market Expiry - Strike (12,000)))*	*Long Call (12,000) Payoff (Outcome - Premium Paid)*	*Strategy Payoff (Long Call + Short Call)*
10,500	0	70	0	-25	45
10,600	0	70	0	-25	45
10,700	0	70	0	-25	45
10,800	0	70	0	-25	45
10,900	0	70	0	-25	45
11,000	0	70	0	-25	45
11,100	0	70	0	-25	45
11,200	0	70	0	-25	45
11,300	0	70	0	-25	45
11,400	0	70	0	-25	45
11,500	0	70	0	-25	45
11,600	0	70	0	-25	45
11,700	0	70	0	-25	45
11,800	0	70	0	-25	45
11,900	100	-30	0	-25	-55
12,000	200	-130	0	-25	-155
12,100	300	-230	100	75	-155
12,200	400	-330	200	175	-155
12,300	500	-430	300	275	-155
12,400	600	-530	400	375	-155
12,500	700	-630	500	475	-155

All the column headings of Table 6.1 are self-explanatory except for those of Column 2 and Column 4.

Column 2 lists the various possible outcomes of the 11,800 short call.

The heading of Column 2 is: Short Call (11,800) Outcome = MAX (0, (Price at Market Expiry – Strike (11,800))).

Thus, for example, if the market expires at 11,400 then the outcome from this leg would be:

The maximum of 0, and the price at market expiry minus the strike price, which is 11,800.
= the maximum of 0, and (11,400 – 11800)
= the maximum or higher of 0, and – 400
= 0.

Column 4 lists the various possible outcomes of the 12,000 long call.

The heading of column 4 is: Long Call (12,000) Outcome = MAX (0, Price at Market Expiry – Strike, which is 12,000).

Column 5 shows the profit / loss scenarios for the 12,000CE which we have bought. For example, if the market expires at 12,400, then the outcome from this leg would be:

The higher of 0, and the price at market expiry minus the strike price, which is 12,000.
= the higher of 0, and (12,400 – 12,000)
= the higher of 0, and 400
= 400.

Table 6.1 shows that our trade would be in profit so long as Nifty stays below 11,800. The maximum profit, as shown by Table 6.1, would be ₹45 × 75 = ₹3,375, which is nothing but the premium you collected. Thus, if Nifty stays below 11,800, you will be in profit, the profit being limited to the premium collected.

On the other hand, if there is an uptrend in the market and Nifty closes above 11,800, you will have a limited loss as shown in Table 6.1.

For example, if Nifty closes at 12,000 then your loss will be ₹155 × 75 = ₹11,625. **This is your maximum possible loss and you can't lose more than this amount even if the market goes higher than 12,000.**

Bull Put Spread

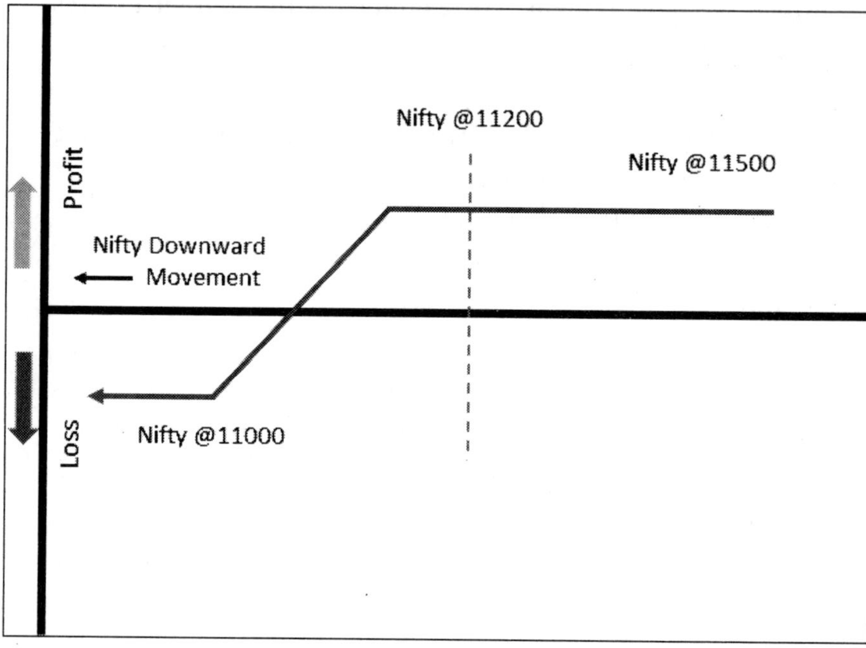

Figure 6.2: Payoff Graph of Bull Put Spread – a two-leg strategy

Bull put spread is used when the trader has a bullish market view.

Suppose Nifty is at 11,500, and you think that it is unlikely to fall below 11,200 in the current expiry. Accordingly, let's assume you sell an OTM 11,200PE (put option) which carries a premium of ₹70. To safeguard yourself, you also buy a far OTM strike. Let's say you buy 11,000PE (put option) at ₹25. Taking Nifty's lot size as 75, let's see what the different profit / loss scenarios would be.

- Market view: Market will not go below a certain level before expiry.
- Legs involved: Two.
- Premium collected by selling 11,200 put option: ₹70 × 75 = ₹5,250.
- Money spent in buying OTM 11,000 put option: ₹25 × 75 = ₹1,875.
- Net premium collected = ₹5,250 - ₹1,875 = ₹3,375.
- Margin required: Around ₹60,000; remember, hedged positions require lesser margin.

Profit / Loss Scenarios

Market Closes on Or Above 11,200

If Nifty closes on or above 11,200, i.e. at or below your OTM PE sell strike price, then both 11,200PE and 11,000PE options will expire worthless, and you get to keep the total premium of ₹3,375.

Market Closes Below 11,000

If the market closes below 11,000 due to a sudden down trend, say it falls to 10,800, your loss will still be limited to the difference between the two strike prices, minus the net premium received at the time of entering the trade. Let's calculate the loss.

Loss on the sell leg = (₹10,800 – ₹11,200) × 75 = ₹30,000.

Profit on the buy leg = (₹11,000 – ₹10,800) × 75 = ₹15,000.

Total payout = -30,000 + 15,000 + 3,375 (premium received)

= - ₹11,625 (loss).

Thus, your maximum loss will be ₹11,625 if the market goes against your view. Also, irrespective of the level to which the market may go against you, your maximum loss will be capped at ₹11,625; you can't lose any more than that. As we will see later, we can lower even this loss by managing our trading position.

To understand the various payoff scenarios from this bull put spread trade, take a look at the pay-off Table 6.2 to see how our profits would be at different market expiries.

Table 6.2

Pay-Off Table for Bull Put Spread

1	2	3	4	5	6
Market Expiry	*Short Put (11,200) Outcome = MAX (0, (Strike (11,200) – Market Expiry)) ₹*	*Short Put (11,200) Payoff (Premium Received – Outcome) ₹*	*Long Put (11,000) Outcome = MAX (0, (Strike (11,000) – Market Expiry)) ₹*	*Long Put (11,000) Payoff (Outcome – Premium Paid) ₹*	*Strategy Payoff (Long Put + Short Put) ₹*
10,500	700	-630	500	475	-155
10,600	600	-530	400	375	-155
10,700	500	-430	300	275	-155
10,800	400	-330	200	175	-155
10,900	300	-230	100	75	-155
11,000	200	-130	0	-25	-155
11,100	100	-30	0	-25	-55
11,200	0	70	0	-25	45
11,300	0	70	0	-25	45
11,400	0	70	0	-25	45
11,500	0	70	0	-25	45
11,600	0	70	0	-25	45
11,700	0	70	0	-25	45
11,800	0	70	0	-25	45
11,900	0	70	0	-25	45
12,000	0	70	0	-25	45
12,100	0	70	0	-25	45
12,200	0	70	0	-25	45
12,300	0	70	0	-25	45
12,400	0	70	0	-25	45
12,500	0	70	0	-25	45

The various column headings of Table 6.2 are self-explanatory except for the headings of Column 2 and Column 4.

Column 2 lists the various possible profit / loss outcomes of shorting the 11,200 put.

The heading of Column 2 reads: Short Put (11,200) Outcome = MAX (0, (Strike (11,200) – Market Expiry)).

Thus, for example, if the market expires at 11,300, then the outcome from this leg would be:

The higher of 0, and the difference between the strike price (11,200) and – the price at market expiry
= the higher of 0, and (11,200 – 11,300)
= the higher of 0, and –100
= 0.

Column 4 lists the various possible profit / loss outcomes of the long 11,000 put.

The heading of Column 4 reads: Long Put (11,000) Outcome = MAX (0, (Strike (11,000) – Market Expiry)).

Thus, for example, if the market expires at 10,700, then the outcome will be:

The higher of 0, and the difference between the strike price (11,000) and the underlying's price at market expiry
= the higher of 0, and (11,000 – 10,700)
= the higher of 0, and 300
= 300.

Table 6.2 reveals that our trade would end in profit so long as Nifty stays above 11,200. The maximum profit, as shown in Table 6.2, would be ₹45 × 75 = ₹3,375, which is nothing but the premium you initially collected. Thus, so long as Nifty stays above 11,200, you will be in profit, limited to the premium collected.

If Nifty falls and closes below 11,200, you will have a limited loss as shown in Table 6.2. For example, if Nifty closes at 11,000 then your loss would be ₹155 × 75 = ₹11,625. This is the maximum loss and you can't lose more than this amount even if the market goes far below the level of 11,000. In other words, this hedged strategy helps to put a cap to your loss.

Iron Condor Strategy

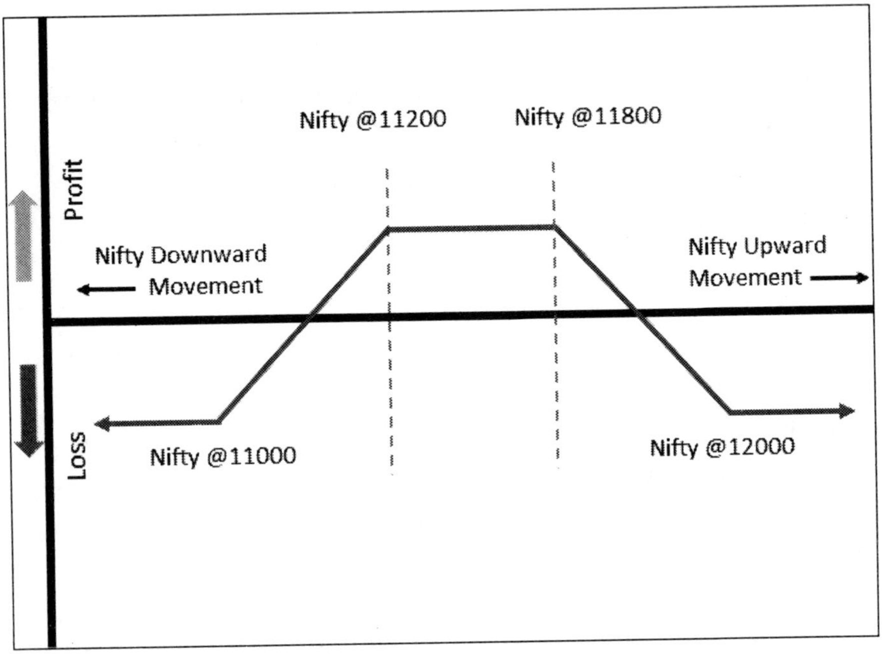

Figure 6.3: Payoff Graph for Iron Condor – a four-leg strategy

Iron Condor is used when the trader has a neutral market view. Iron Condor is a delta neutral strategy, which means that the combined delta of all the legs should be zero. In the case represented in Figure 6.3, the negative and positive deltas of 11,200PE (put option) and 11,800CE (call option) neutralize each other.

Suppose Nifty is at 11,500, and you think that it will remain range bound between 11,200 and 11,800 during the current expiry period. With this view, you might want to sell

11,200PE (put option) and 11,800CE (call option), both available at ₹70 each. To safeguard yourself from any sudden adverse market moves, you would then also have to buy farther OTM strikes on both PE and CE sides. Let's say you buy 11,000PE and 12,000CE at ₹25 each.

In other words, the legs 11,200PE and 11,800CE are sold in order to generate profits. The two OTMs 11,000PE and 12,000CE are bought to limit the losses. Taking Nifty's lot as 75, let's see what the profit and loss scenario would be for this Iron Condor trade.

- Market view: Market will remain range-bound between 11,200 and 11,800.
- Legs involved: Four.
- Premium collected by selling the two options: (₹70 × 75) × 2 = ₹10,500.
- Money spent to buy the two OTM options: (₹25 × 75) × 2 = ₹3,750.
- Net premium collected: ₹10,500 – ₹3,750 = ₹6,750.
- Margin required: Around ₹100,000.

Profit / Loss Scenarios

Market Closes between 11,200 and 11,800

If the market closes anywhere between 11,200 and 11,800, namely between your two sell strikes, then both of the long

OTM positions of PE and CE will end worthless, and you get to keep the total premium you collected, which is ₹6,750.

Market Closes Below 11,000

If the market closes below 11,000 due to an unexpected down move, say it goes to 10,800, your will have a limited loss.

- Loss on the PE sell leg: (₹10,800 – ₹11,200) × 75 = ₹30,000.
- Profit on the PE buy leg: (₹11,000 – ₹10,800) × 75 = ₹15,000.
- Profit on the CE sell leg: This will be equal to the premium received, which is ₹6,750.
- Loss on the CE buy leg: This leg will expire worthless because the spot price is now OTM.
- Total payout = – 30,000 + 15,000 + 6,750 – 0 = – ₹8,250 (loss).

Thus, ₹8,250 will be your maximum loss were the market to go against your view. Irrespective of the level below 11,000 to which Nifty may fall, your maximum loss would stay capped at ₹8,250; you can't lose any more than that. We can lower even this loss by managing our positions, as we shall see in Chapter 8.

Market Closes Above 12,000

Even if the market closes above 12,000 due to a sudden uptrend, say it closes at 12,200, your loss would still be limited. Let's calculate the loss.

- Profit on the PE sell leg: This will be equal to the premium received, which is ₹6,750.
- Loss on the PE buy leg: This leg would expire worthless because the spot price is now OTM.
- Loss on the CE sell leg: (₹11,800 – 12,200) × 75 = ₹30,000.
- Profit on the CE buy leg (₹12,200 – 12,000) × 75 = ₹15,000.
- Total payout = 6750 – 0 – 30,000 + 15,000 = – ₹8,250 (loss).

Thus, ₹8,250 will be your maximum loss even if the market goes against your view. Irrespective of the level to which the market may rise and go against you, your maximum loss will stay limited to ₹8,250, and not a rupee more. We can even lower this loss by managing, namely adjusting, our positions during the trade.

Table 6.3 illustrates the various pay-off scenarios from this strategy for different market expiries. The column headings of Table 6.3 have been abbreviated. The unabbreviated headings are listed below the table.

Table 6.3

Pay-Off Table for the Iron Condor Trade

1	2	3	4	5	6	7	8	9	10
ME	*LP1O*	*LP1P*	*SP1O*	*SP1P*	*SC2O*	*SC2P*	*LC2O*	*LC2P*	*SP*
10,500	500	475	700	-630	0	70	0	-25	-110
10,600	400	375	600	-530	0	70	0	-25	-110
10,700	300	275	500	-430	0	70	0	-25	-110
10,800	200	175	400	-330	0	70	0	-25	-110
10,900	100	75	300	-230	0	70	0	-25	-110
11,000	0	-25	200	-130	0	70	0	-25	-110
11,100	0	-25	100	-30	0	70	0	-25	-10
11,200	0	-25	0	70	0	70	0	-25	90
11,300	0	-25	0	70	0	70	0	-25	90
11,400	0	-25	0	70	0	70	0	-25	90
11,500	0	-25	0	70	0	70	0	-25	90
11,600	0	-25	0	70	0	70	0	-25	90
11,700	0	-25	0	70	0	70	0	-25	90
11,800	0	-25	0	70	0	70	0	-25	90
11,900	0	-25	0	70	100	-30	0	-25	-10
12,000	0	-25	0	70	200	-130	0	-25	-110
12,100	0	-25	0	70	300	-230	100	75	-110
12,200	0	-25	0	70	400	-330	200	175	-110
12,300	0	-25	0	70	500	-430	300	275	-110
12,400	0	-25	0	70	600	-530	400	375	-110
12,500	0	-25	0	70	700	-630	500	475	-110

Legend:

Column-1 – ME: Market Expiry

Column-2 – LP1O: Long Put 1 (11,000) Outcome = MAX (0, (Strike (11,000) – Market Expiry))

Column-3 – LP1P: Long Put 1 (11,000) Payoff (Outcome – Premium Paid)

Column-4 – SP1O: Short Put 1 (11,200) Outcome = MAX (0, (Strike (11,200) – Market Expiry))

Column-5 – SP1P: Short Put 1 (11,200) Payoff (Premium Received – Outcome)
Column-6 – SC2O: Short Call 2 (11,800) Outcome = MAX (0, (Market Expiry – Strike (11,800)))
Column-7 – SC2P: Short Call 2 (11,800) Payoff (Premium Received – Outcome)
Column-8 – LC2O: Long Call 2 (12,000) Outcome = MAX (0, (Market Expiry – Strike (12,000)))
Column-9 – LC2P: Long Call 2 (12,000) Payoff (Outcome – Premium Paid)
Column-10 – SP: Strategy Payoff (Payoff of Long Call 1+ Short Call 1 + Short Call 2 + Long Call 2)

Table 6.3 shows what our profit would be if Nifty stays above 11,200 and below 11,800. As Table 6.3 shows, the maximum profit would be ₹90 × 75 (75 being the lot size of Nifty) = ₹6,750, which is nothing but the premium you collected.

Thus, if Nifty stays between 11,200 and 11,800, you will be in profit, the profit being limited to the premium collected.

If there is a downtrend in the market and Nifty closes below 11,200, you will incur a limited loss, as shown in Table 6.3. For example, if Nifty closes at 11,000, then your loss would be –110 × 75 = ₹8,250. This is the maximum possible loss and you can't lose more than this amount even if the market falls much below 11,000.

If there is an uptrend in the market and Nifty closes above 11,800, you will again incur a limited loss, as shown in Table 6.3. For example, if Nifty closes at 12,000 then your loss would be –110 × 75 = ₹8,250. This is your maximum possible loss and you can not lose more than this amount even if the market were to close above 12,000.

Iron Fly Strategy

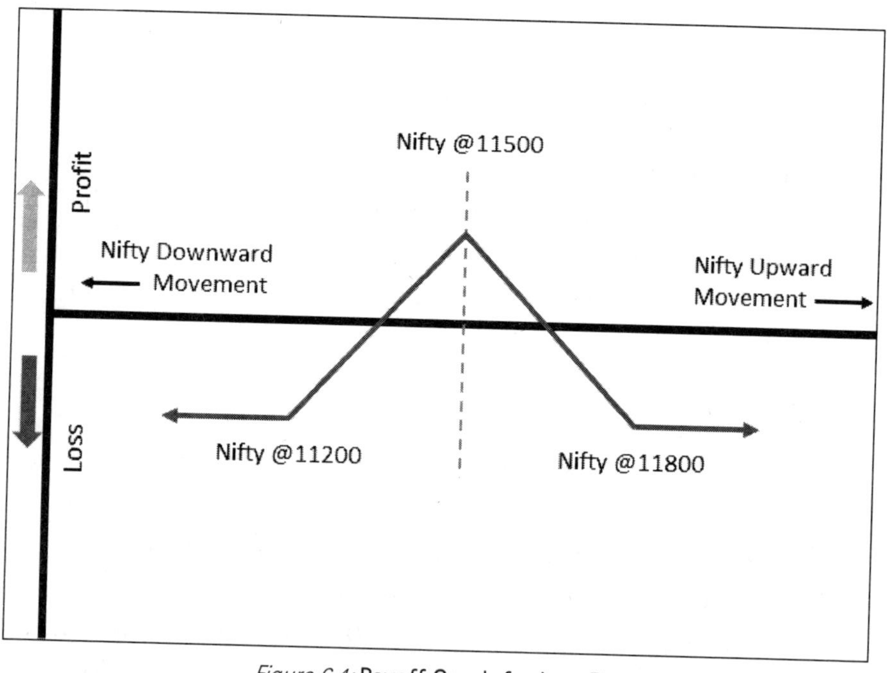

Figure 6.4: Payoff Graph for Iron Fly

Iron Fly strategy is used when the trader has a neutral market view. It's an extension of the Iron Condor strategy that we discussed earlier.

Let's suppose Nifty is at 11,500, and you think that it will remain broadly around the 11,500 level in the current expiry. With this view, you might want to sell an 11,500PE (put option) and an 11,500CE (call option) at ₹120 each. To safeguard yourself even further, you also buy farther OTM strikes. Let's say you buy 11,200PE and 11,800CE at ₹70 each. With the lot size of Nifty being 75, let's see what the profit / loss scenario would be.

- Market view: The market will not move much.
- Legs involved: Four.
- Premium collected by selling the two options: (₹120 × 75) × 2 = ₹18,000.
- Money spent to buy OTM options: (₹70 × 75) × 2 = ₹10,500.
- Net premium collected: ₹18,000 – ₹10,500 = ₹7,500.
- Margin required: Around ₹1,10,000.

Profit / Loss Scenarios

Market Closes at 11,500

If the market closes somewhere around 11,500, then both of the long positions of PE and CE will expire worthless, and you would get to keep the total premium collected, which is ₹7,500.

Market Closes Below 11,500

If the market closes below 11,500 due to a sudden down move, let's say it goes to 11,000, your loss would still be limited. That's the logic and benefit of a hedged strategy. Let's calculate the outcome.

- Loss on the PE sell leg: (11,000 – 11,500) × 75 = ₹37,500.
- Profit on the PE buy leg: (11,200 – 11,000) × 75 = ₹15,000.
- Profit on the CE sell leg: This will be equal to the total premium received, which is ₹7,500.
- Loss on the CE buy leg: This leg will expire worthless because the spot price is now OTM.
- Total payout: – 37,500 + 15,000 – 0 + 7,500 (premium received) = – ₹15,000 (loss).

Thus, ₹15,000 will be the maximum loss even if the market goes against your view. Irrespective of the level to which the market may fall, your maximum loss will remain capped at ₹15,000 only; no more than that. We can reduce even this loss by managing our positions during the trade.

Market Closes Above 11,500

If the market closes above 11,500 due to a sudden upmove, say Nifty goes to 12,000, your loss would still be limited. Let's do the calculation.

- Profit on the PE sell leg: This will be equal to the total premium received which is ₹7,500.
- Loss on the PE buy leg: This leg will expire worthless because the spot price is now OTM.
- Loss on the CE sell leg: (₹11,500 – ₹12,000) × 75 = ₹37,500
- Profit on the CE buy leg: (₹12,000 – ₹11,800) × 75 = ₹15,000
- Total payout = 7,500 + 0 – 37,500 + 15,000 = – ₹15,000 (loss).

Thus, ₹15,000 will be the maximum loss if the market were to go against your view. And irrespective of the level to which the market goes against you, your maximum loss will remain capped at ₹15,000, and no more. You can lower even this loss by intelligently managing your positions, as we shall see in Chapter 8.

Table 6.4 illustrates the various payoff scenarios from this strategy for different market expiries. The column headings of Table 6.4 have been abbreviated. The unabbreviated headings are given below the table.

Table 6.4

Pay-Off Table for Iron Fly Strategy

1	*2*	*3*	*4*	*5*	*6*	*7*	*8*	*9*	*10*
ME	*LP1O*	*LP1P*	*SP1O*	*SP1P*	*SC2O*	*SC2P*	*LC2O*	*LC2P*	*SP*
10,500	700	630	1000	-880	0	120	0	-70	-200
10,600	600	530	900	-780	0	120	0	-70	-200
10,700	500	430	800	-680	0	120	0	-70	-200
10,800	400	330	700	-580	0	120	0	-70	-200
10,900	300	230	600	-480	0	120	0	-70	-200
11,000	200	130	500	-380	0	120	0	-70	-200
11,100	100	30	400	-280	0	120	0	-70	-200
11,200	0	-70	300	-180	0	120	0	-70	-200
11,300	0	-70	200	-80	0	120	0	-70	-100
11,400	0	-70	100	20	0	120	0	-70	0
11,500	0	-70	0	120	0	120	0	-70	100
11,600	0	-70	0	120	100	20	0	-70	0
11,700	0	-70	0	120	200	-80	0	-70	-100
11,800	0	-70	0	120	300	-180	0	-70	-200
11,900	0	-70	0	120	400	-280	100	30	-200
12,000	0	-70	0	120	500	-380	200	130	-200
12,100	0	-70	0	120	600	-480	300	230	-200
12,200	0	-70	0	120	700	-580	400	330	-200
12,300	0	-70	0	120	800	-680	500	430	-200
12,400	0	-70	0	120	900	-780	600	530	-200
12,500	0	-70	0	120	1000	-880	700	630	-200

Legend:

Column-1 – ME: Market Expiry

Column-2 – LP1O: Long Put 1 (11,200) Outcome = MAX (0, (Strike (11,200) – Market Expiry))

Column-3 – LP1P: Long Put 1 (11,200) Payoff (Outcome - Premium Paid)

Column-4 – SP1O: Short Put 1 (11,500) Outcome = MAX (0, (Strike (11,500) - Market Expiry))

Column-5 – SP1P: Short Put 1 (11,500) Payoff (Premium Received - Outcome)

Column-6 – SC2O: Short Call 2 (11,500) Outcome = MAX (0, (Market Expiry - Strike (11,500)))

Column-7 – SC2P: Short Call 2 (11,500) Payoff (Premium Received - Outcome)

Column-8 – LC2O: Long Call 2 (11,800) Outcome = MAX (0, (Market Expiry - Strike (11,800)))

Column-9 – LC2P: Long Call 2 (11,800) Payoff (Outcome - Premium Paid)

Column-10 – SP: Strategy Payoff (Payoff of Long Call 1+ Short Call 1 + Short Call 2 + Long Call2)

Table 6.4 show that the trade would end in profit if the Nifty is around 11,500 at expiry. The maximum profit, as shown in Table 6.4, would be ₹100 × 75 = ₹7,500, which is nothing but the total premium you collected.

So, if Nifty stays at 11,500 at the time of expiry, you will be in profit, limited to the premium collected.

If there is a downtrend in the market, and let's say it closes below 11,500, you will incur a limited loss as shown in Table 6.4. For example, if the Nifty were to close at 11,000, then your loss will be 200 × 75 = ₹15,000. This is your maximum loss — and you can't lose more than this amount even if the market goes well below 11,000.

Conversely, if there is an uptrend in the market and Nifty closes above 11,500, you will again have only a limited loss, as shown in Table 6.4. For example, if Nifty closes at 12,000 then your loss would be 200 × 75 = ₹15,000. This is your maximum loss and you can't lose more than this even if the market rises far above 12,000.

Differences between Naked and Hedged Option Strategies

We are now at the end of this chapter. We have seen the various profit and loss scenarios of a few hedged strategies. In the previous chapter we saw naked option strategies and their outcomes. To re-enforce our understanding, let's compare and contrast the important features of naked and hedged strategies.

Table 6.5

Naked and Hedged Option Strategies Compared

	Naked Strategies	*Hedged Strategies*
Risk Factor	Naked strategies carry unlimited risk potential if the market goes against the trader.	Hedged strategies also carry risk but the risk is clearly pre-defined. Trader cannot lose more than the defined losses in a hedged strategy trade.
Profitability	Profitability is limited to the premiums collected by selling options.	Profitability is limited to the premiums collected by selling options, minus the premium paid for buying farther OTM options. Eventually, in hedged strategies profitability is a little less than naked strategies. But, so is the risk.
Margin Requirements	Since naked strategies carry unlimited loss potential, margin requirements for sellers are higher in such trades.	Since hedged strategies have defined losses, margin requirements for sellers are lower in comparison to naked strategies.

Summary

In this chapter, we discussed some important hedged option strategies from the option seller's perspective. Iron condor is my favorite because of its practical applicability and the ease of managing iron condor trades. If you look closely, iron condor is nothing but a combination of a bear call spread and a bull put spread.

In the next chapter we will learn how to select strikes for the iron condor, and how to adjust them as the trade moves along.

7

~

Selecting Strikes for the Iron Condor

Of all the strategies we have discussed so far, iron condor is the one which most professional option sellers prefer. The reason is simple — iron condor is a seller-oriented strategy. In addition, there are multiple ways one can adjust it for risk and profit even during the trade.

Iron Condor is a delta neutral strategy and this makes it suitable for less volatile stocks or indices. However, if we select our Iron Condor strikes properly, we will sail through profitably even in volatile conditions.

Selecting which strikes to trade is the most crucial aspect of the iron condor strategy, especially the strikes that you propose selling.

Remember, in an iron condor we sell two OTM strikes, and also buy two even more farther OTM strikes.

Now, most retail traders select strikes to sell based on the criterion of open interest (OI). Let's see how this is generally done with the help of an option chain.

Table 7.1

~

Nifty Option Chain

					CALLS										PUTS					
OI	CHNG IN OI	Volume	IV	**LTP**	CHNG	BID Qty	BID Price	ASK Price	ASK Qty	**STRIKE Price**	BID Qty	BID Price	ASK Price	ASK Qty	CHNG	**LTP**	IV	Volume	CHNG IN OI	OI
522	131	311	28.49	**441.75**	-123.55	675	411.20	416.10	75	**11,100**	1,725	14.65	14.80	1,350	6.10	**14.75**	30.45	74,883	-1,650	10,940
149	115	235	32.86	**365.00**	-162.75	600	365.00	365.50	375	**11,150**	300	17.40	17.55	1,275	7.45	**17.40**	29.20	21,305	120	3,005
850	-29	584	32.63	**317.00**	-152.50	375	319.50	321.80	150	**11,200**	750	21.45	21.60	75	9.90	**21.50**	37.94	1,51,587	1,098	18,445
92	56	139	30.56	**275.00**	-148.40	75	276.55	278.95	75	**11,250**	150	27.35	27.50	600	13.85	**27.45**	26.84	38.823	-35	5,939
1,908	-522	3,119	29.10	**234.25**	-141.35	75	234.55	236.40	150	**11,300**	375	36.40	36.60	150	20.10	**36.50**	26.17	2,34,165	748	22,536
264	-2	465	26.63	**195.05**	-133.55	75	195.15	197.00	375	**11,350**	150	47.15	47.45	150	27.60	**47.40**	25.33	89,422	-1,363	6,451
3,754	-103	7,160	27.23	**159.60**	-123.15	75	159.05	159.90	75	**11,400**	450	61.25	61.65	600	36.75	**61.50**	24.55	2,95,117	-851	23,926
1,864	93	2,198	26.54	**128.40**	-111.35	75	128.20	128.95	75	**11,450**	225	78.90	79.30	150	47.95	**78.65**	23.80	1,15,585	-470	7,677
18,390	4,363	52,770	25.54	**99.65**	-98.10	75	99.35	99.70	1,650	**11,500**	75	100.60	101.00	600	61.25	**100.35**	23.16	4,52,957	-2,479	34,286
5,436	3,499	39,974	24.87	**76.20**	-82.30	150	76.00	76.20	75	**11,550**	150	126.50	127.00	75	77.70	**127.00**	22.50	1,80,632	2,711	10,594
31,314	13,816	2,26,286	24.47	**57.80**	-64.40	225	57.60	57.80	75	**11,600**	150	158.00	158.65	75	94.60	**157.80**	22.01	4,55,108	-6,637	28,407
12,018	3,939	1,17,937	24.07	**42.35**	-48.70	75	42.20	42.40	600	**11,650**	75	191.20	192.35	225	110.60	**192.35**	21.30	1,52,209	-2,954	3,771
33,066	11,511	3,73,239	23.89	**30.65**	-33.80	225	30.55	30.70	450	**11,700**	75	231.40	232.00	75	125.70	**230.85**	20.82	3,09,234	1,941	10,185
15,934	3,907	2,05,135	23.88	**22.40**	-20.65	225	22.25	22.40	1,800	**11,750**	300	270.75	272.05	75	137.40	**271.45**	19.97	99,558	1,129	2,052
42,143	18,274	4,95,617	23.89	**15.80**	-11.40	450	15.80	15.90	225	**11,800**	75	316.95	318.25	75	150.00	**316.30**	19.82	1,23,949	1,873	4,099
14,707	3,133	1,82,362	24.10	**11.35**	-4.85	75	11.30	11.40	1,875	**11,850**	75	360.90	362.75	75	154.25	**360.50**	19.56	13,306	137	472
32,827	11,198	3,72,215	24.56	**8.50**	-1.25	8,550	8.40	8.45	1,875	**11,900**	75	409.45	410.50	150	159.65	**409.85**	-	22,857	510	1,085
9,950	1,191	1,23,271	25.12	**6.20**	0.05	1,200	6.15	6.25	2,100	**11,950**	150	455.85	461.15	75	161.45	**459.40**	34.23	476	84	150
43,069	9,895	3,17,814	26.16	**4.95**	0.50	1,800	4.95	5.00	16,200	**12,000**	225	504.45	507.10	75	161.80	**504.55**	-	5,364	231	1,122

The option chain in Table 7.1 indicates that Nifty is currently trading at 11,500. Now, generally, people look for such out-of-the-money (OTM) CE and PE options where OI is the highest. Nifty's option chain in Table 7.1 indicates that OTM strikes with the maximum OI are 11,400PE and 12,000CE. This is where the maximum number of option sellers, including big institutions, have written options. If you want to go ahead and give this approach a try, you can evaluate it with the help of paper trading. I prefers a different approach to selecting the strikes to sell, based on statistical measures. To be precise, we would be using standard deviation to select our strikes.

Understanding Standard Deviation (SD)

Standard deviation (SD) is a measure of an asset's volatility, and it measures how tightly, or otherwise, data is bunched around a mean, i.e. an average.

There are various studies on this subject that suggest that for a stock or an index there exists in a given period of time:

- 68.2% probability of it closing between its +1SD and –1SD;
- 95.4% probability of it closing between +2SD and –2SD;
- 99.7% probability of it closing between +3SD and –3SD;

The SD, in turn, will vary depending on the time remaining to expiry and the instrument's volatility.

- The farther away the expiry date is, the higher is the standard deviation.
- The higher the volatility, the higher is the standard deviation.

Figure 7.1 graphically demonstrates that, there are 68.2% chances that the stock price movement will remain between –1SD to +1SD in a given period of time.

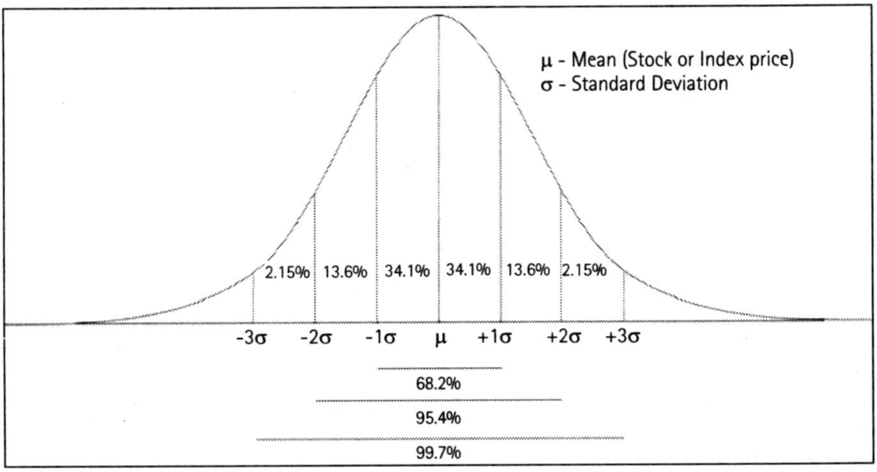

Figure 7.1: The standard deviation of a stock or index

We will not consider using 2SD and 3SD strikes since such strikes will be far too out of the money and won't yield much gain on a regular basis. Instead, we will focus on 1SD strikes which statistically give us a 68% chance of winning — and even if things do go wrong, we can always manage our ongoing trade positions. In other words, generally speaking 1SD is the range where we want to sell out-of-the-money strikes in our Iron Condor.

While performing our SD calculations we will be making use of the strike's implied volatility (IV). You would recall that implied volatility was discussed briefly in Chapter 3.

Let's now see how the 1SD of an index or a stock is calculated.

Calculating 1SD of NIFTY

The next question is — how to calculate the standard deviation for an index or a stock. Let's see how we can calculate 1SD for Nifty.

- **Instrument:** NIFTY.
- **Lot Size:** 75.
- **Current Date:** 31 August 2020.
- **Current Expiry:** 24 September 2020.
- **Latest Traded Price (LTP):** 11,500.

- **Time to Expiry (TTE)**: 19 days, considering only market working days.
- **ATM Call IV**: 25.54 and 24.87; please refer to the Nifty Option Chain in Table 7.1.
- **ATM Put IV**: 23.16 and 22.50; please refer to the Nifty Option Chain in Table 7.1.
- **Cumulative Implied Volatility (CIV)**: (25.54 + 24.87 + 23.16 + 22.50) ÷ 4 = 24.01
- **Daily Volatility (DV)**: CIV (24.01) ÷ square root of 252 trading days of a calendar year, considering only working days: (SQRT (252)) = 1.51
- **Monthly Volatility (MV)**: DV (1.51) × square root of TTE (SQRT (19)) = 6.59
- **–1 Standard Deviation**: LTP (11500) – (LTP (11500) × MV% (6.59%)) = 10741.83
- **+1 Standard Deviation**: LTP (11500) + (LTP (11500) × MV% (6.59%)) = 12258.17

With the above calculation we have obtained a range for 1SD which suggests that as per statistics there is a 68.2% profitably that Nifty will move between 10,741.83 and 12,258.17 till the end of the current monthly expiry. If you check Nifty's actual historical prices for that period from the NSE website, you will find that Nifty closed on 10,805.55 on 24 September 2020 (*see* Table 7.2).

Table 7.2

Nifty on 24 September 2020

Historical Index Data

Select the index you want:

Select Index: NIFTY 50

Select a time period: 24-09-2020 To 24-09-2020

Get Data

Historical Data for NIFTY 50						
For the period 24-09-2020 to 24-09-2020						
Date	Open	High	Low	Close	Shares Traded	Turnover (₹ Cr)
24-Sep-2020	11011.00	11015.30	10790.20	10805.55	706139506	33623.71

Download file in csv format

The historical data can be seen on the NSE website on the following link – https://www1.nseindia.com/products/content/equities/indices/historical_index_data.htm

So, if we had sold only these strikes on 31 August, namely 10,700 PE and 12,300 CE, which is a short strangle scenario, we would certainly have been in profit.

If we wanted to further safeguard ourselves then we must buy farther OTM strikes, for example you could buy 10,500 PE and 12,500 CE. That would create an Iron Condor.

Calculating 1SD of SBI

Now let's calculate 1SD for State Bank of India.

- **Instrument:** SBIN.
- **Lot Size:** 3,000.
- **Current Date:** 5 January 2021.
- **Current Expiry:** 28 January 2021.
- **Latest Traded Price (LTP):** 281.40.
- **Time to Expiry (TTE):** 17 days (considering only working days).
- **ATM Call IV:** 39.17 and 39.52.
- **ATM Put IV:** 41.54 and 42.17.
- **Cumulative Implied Volatility (CIV):** (39.17 + 39.52 + 41.54 + 42.17) ÷ 4 = 40.60
- **Daily Volatility (DV):** CIV (40.60) ÷ square root of 252, being the nature of trading days in a calendar year, considering only working days: (SQRT (252)) = 2.56
- **Monthly Volatility (MV):** DV (2.56) × square root of TTE (SQRT (17)) = 10.55
- **–1 Standard Deviation:** LTP (281.40) – (LTP (281.40) × MV% (10.55%)) = 251.73

- **+1 Standard Deviation:** LTP (281.40) + (LTP (281.40) × MV% (10.55%)) = 311.07

With the above calculation we have obtained a range of 1SD which suggests a 68.2% probability that SBIN price will range between ₹251.73 and ₹311.07 till the end of the current expiry. If one were to check the historical prices of SBIN from the NSE website, you will discover that SBIN closed on ₹282.35 on 28 January 2021 (*see* Table 7.3).

So if we had sold only these strikes on 5 January, namely 250PE and 310CE, which is a short strangle, we would certainly have been in profits. If we want to safeguard ourselves even more, then we must buy farther OTM strikes; for example you could have bought 230PE and 330CE, to make an Iron Condor.

Table 7.3

SBIN as on 28 January 2021

Security-wise Archives (Equities) Full Download

Get historical data for: Security-wise Price volume & Deliverable position data Enter symbol: SBIN Select series : EQ

Period: For past: OR Select a Time Period: 28-01-2021 To 28-01-2021

Data for SBIN - EQ from Jan 28, 2021 to Jan 28, 2021

Symbol	Series	Date	Prev Close	Open Price	High Price	Low Price	Last Price	Close Price	VWAP	Total Traded Quantity	Turnover ₹	No. of Trades	Deliverable Qty	% Dly Qt to Traded Qty
SBIN	EQ	28-Jan-2021	275.65	271.90	283.35	269.50	282.90	282.35	277.04	4,87,17,297	13,49,66,76,252.60	2,80,797	1,17,29,218	24.08

The above historical data can be seen on NSE website on the following link: https://www1.nseindia.com/products/content/equities/equities/eq_security.htm

Calculating 1SD of ITC

Now let's calculate 1SD for ITC.

- **Instrument:** ITC.
- **Lot Size:** 3,200.
- **Current Date:** 5 January 2021.
- **Current Expiry:** 28 January 2021.
- **Latest Traded Price (LTP):** 211.45.
- **Time to Expiry (TTE):** 17 days (considering only working days).
- **ATM Call IV:** 32.42 and 33.33.
- **ATM Put IV:** 33.53 and 33.09.
- **Cumulative Implied Volatility (CIV):** (32.42 + 33.33 + 33.53 + 33.09) ÷ 4 = 33.09
- **Daily Volatility (DV):** CIV (33.09) ÷ square root of 252 trading days of a calendar year (considering only working days): (SQRT (252)) = 2.08
- **Monthly Volatility (MV):** DV (2.08) × square root of TTE (SQRT (17)) = 8.60
- **–1 Standard Deviation:** LTP (211.45) – (LTP (211.45) × MV% (8.60%)) = 193.28
- **+1 Standard Deviation:** LTP (211.45) + (LTP (211.45) × MV% (8.60%)) = 229.62

Table 7.4

ITC as on 28 January 2021

Security-wise Archives (Equities)

Full Download

Get historical data for: Security-wise Price volume & Deliverable position data Enter symbol: ITC Select series : EQ

Period: For past: please select OR Select a Time Period: 28-01-2021 To 28-01-2021 Get Data

Data for ITC - EQ from Jan 28, 2021 to Jan 28, 2021 Download file in csv format

Symbol	Series	Date	Prev Close	Open Price	High Price	Low Price	Last Price	Close Price	VWAP	Total Traded Quantity	Turnover ₹	No. of Trades	Deliverable Qty	% Dly Qt to Traded Qty
ITC	EQ	28-Jan-2021	210.65	209.25	211.00	205.75	206.85	206.60	208.22	2,21,31,983	4,60,83,95,814.05	1,31,065	74,41,957	33.63

Above historical data can be seen on NSE website on the following link - https://www1.nseindia.com/products/content/equities/equities/eq_security.htm

With the above calculation we get a range of 1SD which suggests that statistically there is a 68.2% probability that ITC will close between ₹193.28 and ₹229.62 at the end of the current expiry. If you were to check historical prices of ITC from the NSE website, you will be surprised that ITC did actually close at ₹206.60 on 28 January 2021 (*see* Table 7.4). So if we had sold only these strikes, namely 190PE and 230CE, on 5 January, incidentally, this is a short strangle, we would certainly have been in profit. If we had wanted to safeguard ourselves then we would have bought farther OTM strikes, for example bought 170PE and 250CE, and this will make an Iron Condor.

Summary

In this chapter we have learnt how to choose our strikes for an iron condor.

For one, we can always go with the sentiment of the market and choose strikes where there is maximum open interest (OI) in the option chain.

Alternatively, we can choose our strikes on the basis of statistics. While I have provided three examples where LTP on expiry remained within the calculated 1SD range, if you examine historical data from NSE, you will find that most of the time the expiry LTP does indeed fall within 1SD range. And whenever the price breaches the 1SD range, we can adjust our positions mid-trade. How to carry out such adjustments is what we will learn next in Chapter 8.

8

~

Managing Ongoing Iron Condor Trades

In this chapter we will learn how you can manage ongoing Iron Condor trades when the trade doesn't go as per your plan, or the market is not moving as per your expectation. Managing, or adjusting, an ongoing options trade position is a crucial skill while every trader must master; otherwise in a volatile market situation you may you end up with losses even if you employ a hedged strategy such as Iron Condor.

Suppose you have taken a trade position in accordance with the 1SD (one standard deviation) criterion as explained in the previous chapter. As the index starts to move in either direction, delta of the threatened side will also start to change. Consequently, the overall position will not remain delta neutral any more. Typically, small and individual traders start to close their positions, even at a loss, once such a move becomes prominent. In such situation, before closing your trade positions in loss, you should always evaluate if you can instead profitably manage the position.

Thumb Rules for Managing Iron Condor Trades

There are two rules of thumb regarding managing iron condor trades:

- For highly volatile stocks, for example State Bank of India (NSE: SBIN), you should adjust your positions only if the last traded price (LTP) of the stock reaches within 5% of the strike price. Nothing needs to be done so long as the LTP is beyond 5% of the strike price.
- For less volatile stocks, say, for example ITC, you should adjust our positions only if the LTP of the stock reaches within 3% of the strike price. Nothing needs to be done so long as the LTP of a less volatile stock is more than 3% distant from the option's strike price.

Let us now understand these rules with the help of an example.

Suppose, LTP of SBIN is ₹200, and you have initiated your Iron Condor for the current expiry as follows:

- Bought 10 lots of 160PE;
- Sold 10 lots 180PE;
- Sold 10 lots 220CE;
- Bought 10 lots of 240CE.

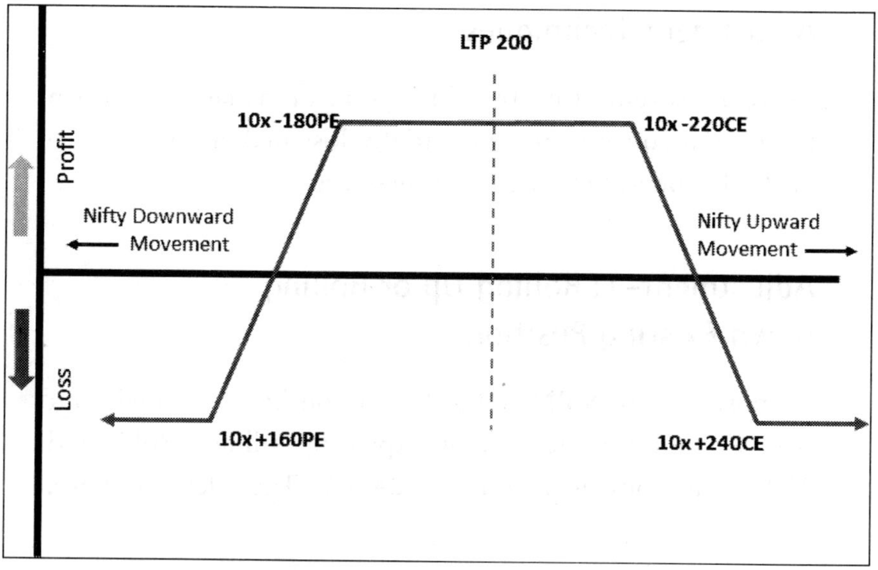

Figure 8.1: Payoff Graph of SBIN Iron Condor

Let's quickly calculate how far the sell strikes are from the LTP.

- 220CE: ((220-200) ÷ 200) × 100 = 10%
- 180PE: ((180-200) ÷ 200) × 100 = – 10%

If SBIN starts to move and goes up from ₹200 to ₹210, it would then be ((210-200)/200) × 100 = 5% from the 220CE strike. At the start of the trade, the distance was 10%. When SBIN moves up and breaches ₹210, then as per our rule we must adjust our position since it is a volatile stock and it may show big movements. We can do a similar calculation if SBIN starts to move lower.

Adjustment Techniques

There are several ways by which you can manage your open trades and convert your potentially loss making trades into profitable ones. Let's see what these are.

Adjustment-1: Rolling Up or Rolling Down Existing Positions

Suppose LTP of SBIN is ₹200, and you have initiated your Iron Condor for the current expiry by selling 180PE and 220CE, and buying 160PE and 240CE. Then, let's suppose,

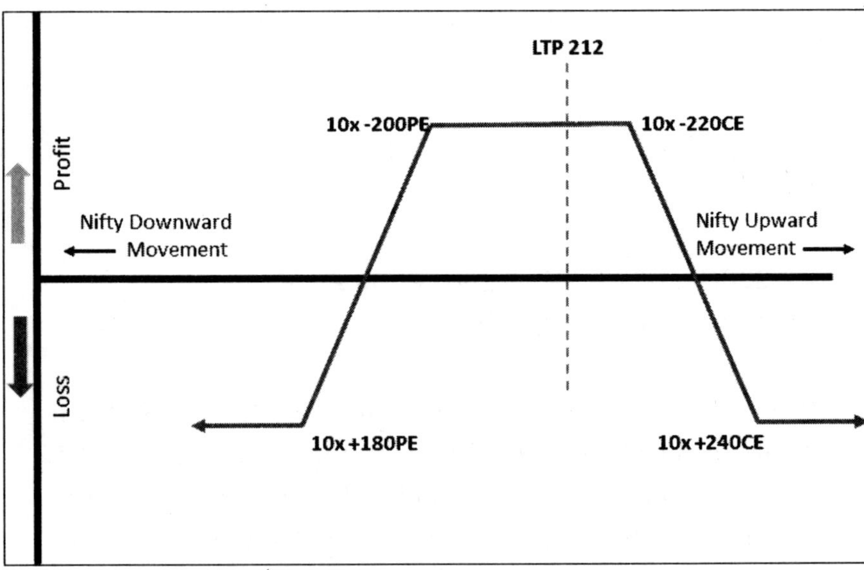

Figure 8.2: Payoff Graph for Adjustment-1 to the Iron Condor trade

along comes some positive news and SBIN starts to move up. We should leave our position untouched so long as SBIN's price remains below ₹210, i.e. so long as it is more than 5% away from 220CE. Once the price rises above ₹210, like in the graph in Figure 8.2, where it has reached ₹212, we can roll-up our PE positions. Rolling up means closing 160PE and 180PE positions completely, and instead buying 180PE and selling 200PE, instead. Delta will then again become close to neutral if we follow this strategy of adjusting our position.

A similar adjustment can be applied if there is a sharp fall in SBIN. In that case, you will have to roll-down your CE positions.

Pros

By rolling up, the trader will collect higher premium since the PE side will be a profit making one once the script moves higher.

Cons

This is an aggressive adjustment strategy and you should be cautious while using it. If SBIN reverses sharply from ₹212, the trader will then have to manage the PE positions quickly.

When to Use this Adjustment

This adjustment should be used when there are sufficient indicators, or significant news, indicating a directional movement, whether positive or negative.

Adjustment-2: Doubling Your Non-Threatened Position

This adjustment is less aggressive than the earlier one, and it doesn't involve rolling up your PE positions. Instead, it involves doubling your non-threatened positions. In our example that would mean doubling the PE positions, from 10

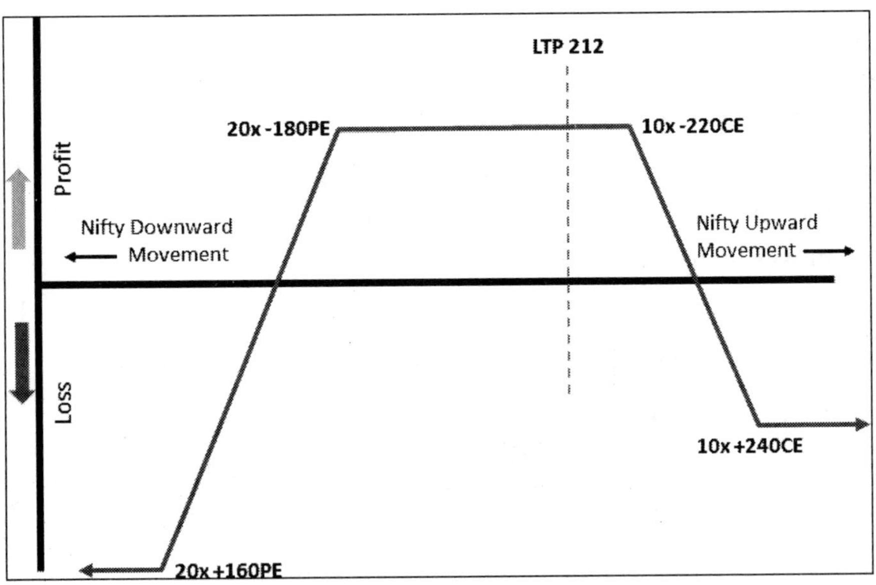

Figure 8.3: Payoff Graph for Doubling of Non-Threatened Position

lots to 20 lots, as per the graph in Figure 8.3. By doing this, your capital would be at greater risk if there is a sharp reversal, but Delta will again approach neutral. This approach will require higher margin money than Adjustment-1. The same kind of graph can be plotted if there is a directional movement towards the lower PE side, and then you might need to increase your exposure on the CE side.

Pros

By increasing one's position on the non-threatened side, the trader will collect higher premium. Also, since your non-threatened side is at the same strike as before, it will give you time to think before making any further adjustment.

Cons

This adjustment is not as aggressive as Adjustment-1 where we rolled-up our positions, but it has more downside risk if the market moves down quickly, since your position is bigger after the adjustment. Should SBIN reverse sharply from ₹212, then the trader will have to manage the PE positions quickly.

When to Use this Adjustment

This adjustment should be used when we are not sure if the directional movement will sustain for much longer.

Adjustment-3: Putting Additional Capital in the Same Expiry Cycle on the Threatened Side

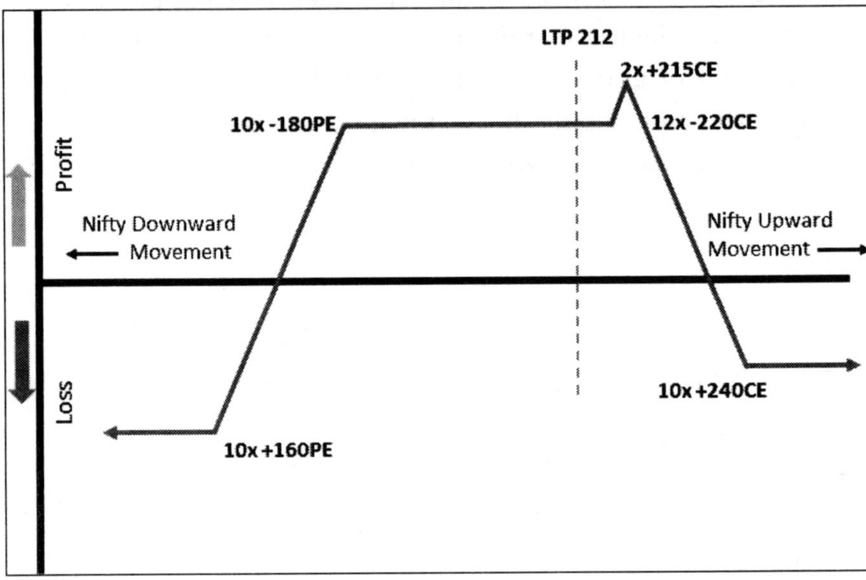

Figure 8.4: Payoff Graph for Putting Additional Capital in the Same Expiry Cycle on the Threatened Side

In the first two adjustments we can collect additional premium by rolling-up our position (Adjustment-1), or by increasing our exposure on the non-threatened side (Adjustment-2), respectively. We consider Adjustment-1 and Adjustment-2 to be aggressive adjustments where the trader collects additional premium. Adjustment-3 is rather defensive in nature. On the other hand, here we buy a few long calls, and also add more short calls in the existing CE position. This will cost us money, but our capital at risk will be reduced on the threatened side of the position.

Let us again consider our Iron Condor with long 160PE, short 180PE, short 220CE, and long 240CE with 10 lots of each leg, and with SBIN trading at ₹200. If the price moves up to ₹212, as per the graph in Figure 8.4, we can leave our non-threatened side, i.e. long 160PE and short 180PE as it is. On the threatened CE side, we can sell 2 more lots, making the portion 12 lot short 220CE. To balance this additional selling, we must buy 2 lots with strike between SBIN current price, which is ₹212, and the short call which is 220. So, as the graph in Figure 8.4 suggests, we can buy 2 lots of 215CE. To do so, the trader will have to pay a premium to buy 215CE which will impact the total profitability of the strategy but the capital at risk will also be reduced if SBIN moves even higher from ₹212. Please note that this adjustment will cost the trader money because selling 2 additional lots of 220CE will not fetch that much premium, as the trader will have to pay for buying 2 lots of 215CE. We know that strikes which are near to the ATM will have higher Delta and hence they will have more premium. This is the reason 215CE will have more premium than 220CE, considering the LTP is at ₹212

Pros

Capital at risk on the threatened side will reduce and the position will become delta neutral again.

Cons

This adjustment will cost us money since buying a CE closer to the LTP is always more expensive than selling a CE farther from the LTP.

When to Use this Adjustment

We can use this adjustment strategy when the market is overbought — in case the market is moving up, or oversold in case the market is moving down, and there is high possibility of a quick reversal. You can determine if the market is overbought or oversold by using the indicators which were discussed in Chapter 4. You don't want to disturb your non-threatened side in this case; rather, you are putting additional capital on the threatened side to make this temporary adjustment.

Adjustment-4: Putting Additional Capital in the Next Expiry Cycle on the Threatened Side

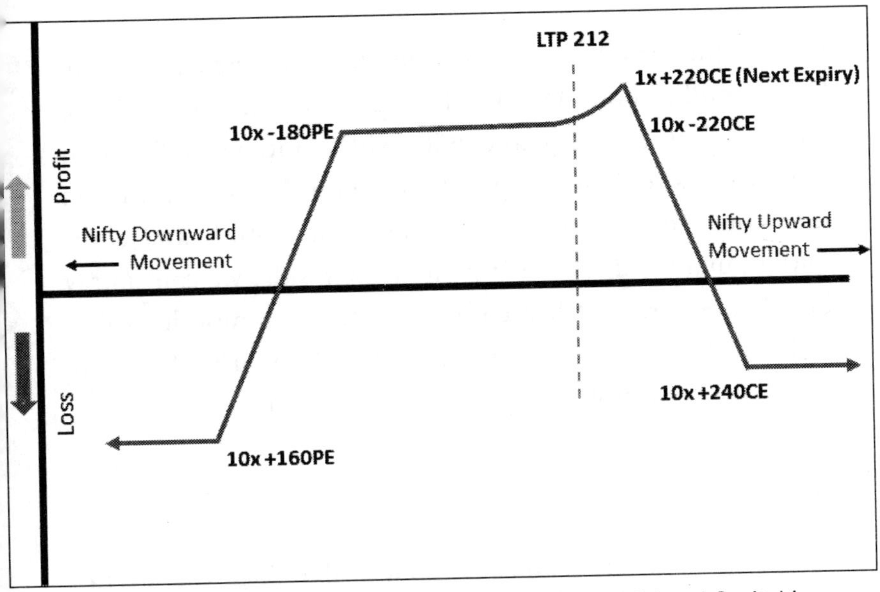

Figure 8.5: Payoff Graph for Adjustment-4: Putting Additional Capital in the Next Expiry Cycle on the Threatened Side

If the stock is moving rather quickly, then instead of buying a call option of the same expiry, you could consider buying a call option of the next expiry. Since the Delta will be much higher for the next expiry, it will provide a good cushion on the threatened side of the position. Basically, this is a temporary adjustment measure which can also be profitable if the stock continues to move up. Such an adjustment will help reduce your losses from the short CE position. Please remember, if the market is going up, short PE positions are already making money.

Let's again consider our Iron Condor of August expiry with long 160PE, short 180PE, short 220CE and long 240CE with 10 lots each leg and with SBIN trading at ₹200. If SBIN moves to ₹212, as per the graph in Figure 8.5 we can leave our non-threatened side, i.e. long 160PE and short 180PE, unaltered. On the threatened CE side, we can simply buy 1 lot 220CE of September, i.e. the next month expiry. Delta will be higher for the next month expiry which will move quickly if SBIN continues to move up from ₹212.

Pros

This is an easy adjustment which will reduce the overall Delta. We use it if there is a lot of volatility in the stock, and we need to reduce the position's Vega.

Cons

This adjustment will cost us money since we are buying a call option of the next expiry.

When to Use this Adjustment

We can use this adjustment strategy if there is high volatility in the market. In such cases, the market can move up or down very quickly, and we need to be able to cut our losses.

Adjustment-5: Putting Additional Capital on Both Legs in the Next Expiry Cycle on the Threatened Side

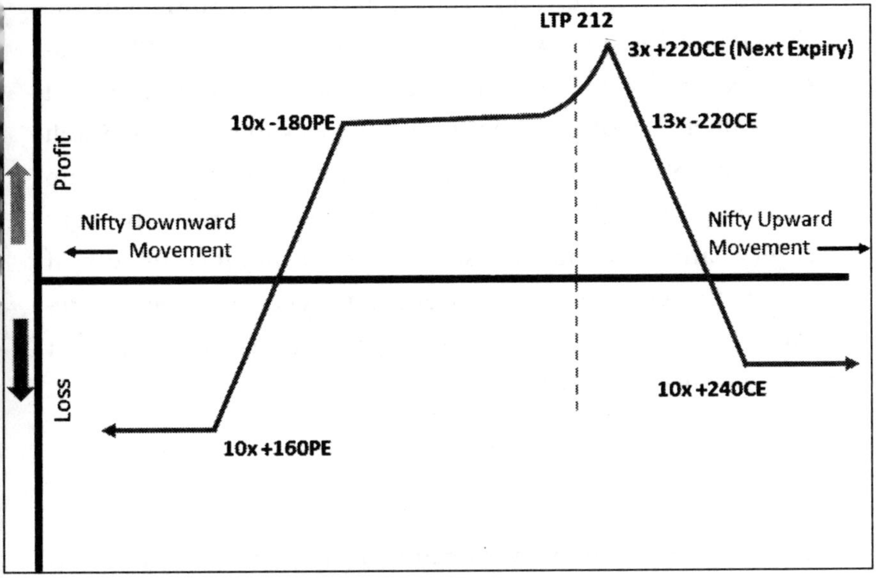

Figure 8.6: Payoff Graph for Adjustment-5: Putting Additional Capital on Both Legs in the Next Expiry Cycle on the Threatened Side

Before considering this adjustment, we need to remind ourselves of the time value of option premiums and the option Greek Theta, which was explained thoroughly in Chapter 3. We know that longer the time to expiry, higher will be both Theta and the option premium.

Let's again consider our Iron Condor of August expiry with long 160PE, short 180PE, short 220CE and long 240CE with having each leg and with 10 lots and with SBIN trading at ₹200. Now, if the price moves to ₹212, as shown in the graph in Figure 8.6 we can leave alone our non-threatened side, i.e. long 160PE and short 180PE. On the threatened CE side, we can short 3 more lots of 220CE August expiry. To balance this, we can buy 3 lots of 220CE of September, i.e. of next month expiry, as shown in the graph in Figure 8.6. Here we are expecting the price to move up quickly and we have bought a few lots of CE of the next expiry, and subsequently sold the same number of lots of CE in the current expiry. Delta and Vega will be get reduced, and we will have a nice profit curve if the market closes near the short CE call.

Pros

This is a very nice way of reducing both Delta and Vega. This adjustment will lead to profits if the market expires below the short CE positions.

Cons

If the market reverses from its current level, our trading position will be in loss since we have bought CE of the next expiry which has a higher Delta. So if the market reverses, 220CE leg of September expiry will contribute most to the losses.

When to Use this adjustment

This strategy is good if you are close to expiry, and you think that despite the market trending, it will likely expire at around its current level itself. If your assumption is correct, you will be sitting on huge profit at expiry by using this adjustment.

Adjustment-6: Close Existing Positions and Create a Fresh Delta Neutral Position

This is a simple adjustment where you close your existing position entirely and create a fresh delta neutral position. We may have to make this adjustment if the market is very volatile in both upward and downward directions. In such extremely volatile situations, it's always better to close one's entire positions and start afresh with new legs. If the market is in an uptrend the closing of CE positions, will lead to a loss since the LTP has moved up; but you will collect premium on the PE side. Similarly, if the market is in a downtrend, you will be in a loss in closing your PE positions, since the LTP has moved down; but you will collect premium on the CE side.

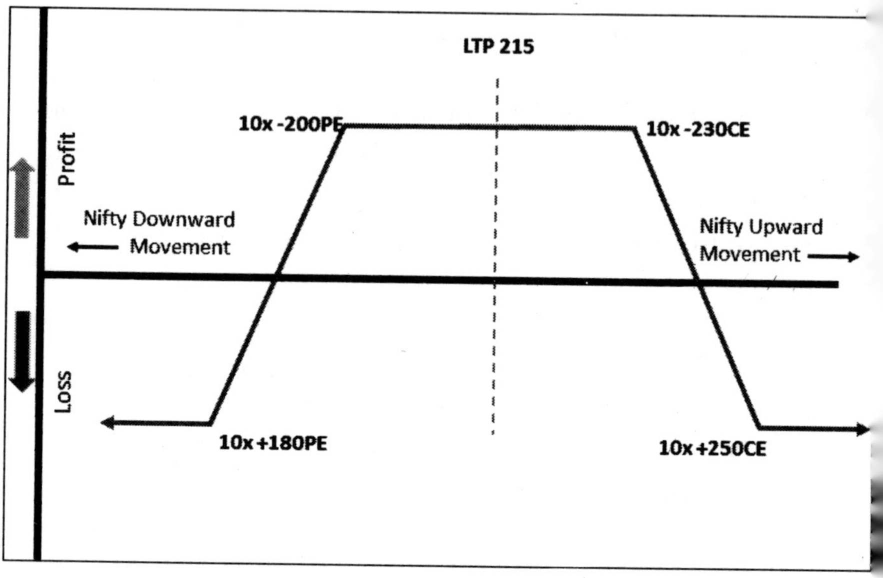

Figure 8.7: Payoff Graph for Adjustment-6: Close Existing Positions and Create a Fresh Delta Neutral Position

Pros

Since you will start afresh, your position will be delta neutral again.

Cons

If the market has moved up — or down — quickly, this adjustment will cost you money since you will lose more on the threatened side than you would earn on the non-threatened side.

When to Use this Adjustment

This adjustment can be used if the anticipated trading range is broken entirely and the market is also extremely volatile. What does broken trading range mean? Suppose you have started your trade with 1SD positions and this range is broken, then starting afresh might be a good idea with new 1SD positions.

When to Exit a Trade Instead of Making Adjustments

Traders should always keep an eye on their defined stop loss in a trade. For example, if your stop loss is 5% of margin money, and that 5% has been breached, you should completely close that trade without attempting any further adjustments.

On the other hand, if your stop loss hasn't been hit, you can go ahead with the adjustment route. If the market remains as per your expectation, you will make money using the appropriate adjustment but if the market moves contrary to your expectation, and your stop loss has been hit, you should get out of the trade completely.

Summary

In this chapter we have learnt some important adjustment techniques which come in handy when things are not going according to your initial anticipation. Adjustments always cost additional money — by way of margin — but will also either reduce your loss, or increase your potential profit, from the trade. A few of the adjustment strategies we discussed are aggressive, while some others are defensive in nature. In Chapter 9, we will review a few real trades before finalizing a roadmap for earning a monthly income of ₹20,000.

~

9

~

My Real-Life Trades

We started our learning journey of options trading from the very basics, namely by trying to understand options terminology and concepts. After that we saw how option selling is more profitable than buying options. We also saw a few of the most widely used options trading strategies — and how to manage, i.e. make adjustments, mid-trade when required. I believe this is sufficient knowledge for you to start your options trading journey.

Start Your Trading Journey with Paper Trading

I would urge you to first try paper trading using all the knowledge you have gained till now. Paper trading is nothing but methodically recording all your hypothetical trading actions on paper, as though you are actually executing the trade. Once you close the trade on paper, you can actually calculate your profit / loss using mark-to-market (MTM). We discussed MTM in detail while discussing the concept of margin money. Once you feel confident about your approach, you can begin real-life trading, with limited capital and small trading positions to start with.

~

To help you get a feel of real-life trading I am sharing below the actual trades I took during the three-month period from July 2020 to September 2020. All of these trades involved the use of State Bank of India (NSE: SBIN) options. We will go through each of these trades and try to understand what I did, what was the rationale behind what I did, the outcome of each trade, and what were the lessons learnt. But, first, let's understand the trading system that I used.

The Trading System

Every individual trader is different. His or her trading style is different, risk capacities are different and, so, the market outcomes, namely the profit or loss, arising from their trade positions are also different. You need to have a system of your own based on the amount of trading capital you have, your temperament, your trading knowledge, and your risk tolerance. Thereafter, you need to be very disciplined and follow your system most strictly. When I talk of a system, it means a simple set of rules that you can follow when you trade. Over the years I have developed my own system which I try to adhere to. Whenever I deviated from my rules, it has led to the bitter taste of loss.

My trading system is as follows.

Profit Target and Trade Closing

I always close the trade once I have made 75% of the maximum possible profit from it. Alternately, I close the trade one week before the expiry day, whichever occur earlier. What does this mean, and why do I follows this rule?

Let's try to answer this, using the following illustration.

- Stock: XYZ
- Current price: ₹100
- Lot size: 3,000.

Now, let's suppose I take the following positions to make an Iron Condor.

- Sell 90PE at ₹4.00. Premium collected = 3,000 × 4.00 = ₹12,000.
- Sell 110CE at ₹3.50. Premium collected = 3,000 × 3.50 = ₹10,500.
- Buy 70PE at ₹2.00. Premium paid = 3,000 × 2.00 = ₹6,000.
- Buy 130CE at ₹1.50. Premium paid = 3,000 × 1.50 = ₹4,500.
- Total premium collected = ₹22,500.
- Total premium paid = ₹10,500.
- Maximum profit potential of this trade = ₹22,500 – ₹10,500 = ₹12,000.

So the maximum profit potential of this trade is ₹12,000 as shown above. Instead of aiming to capture the entire potential profit of ₹12,000, I would opt to close my position when I reach 75% of ₹12,000. Thus I would close my position, with around ₹9,000 profit. To get 100% of the profit, you need to wait for the option premium to become zero. That happens only on the day of expiry at around 3:00 p.m.; till then, options tend to have some premium remaining. When the option premium become zero, the option obviously becomes worthless (*see* Figure 9.1).

Figure 9.1 represents the premium time decay which is nothing but a representation of how the option premium reduces when we move towards expiry. The closer we get to expiry, the faster the option premium starts to lose its value. Looking at the option premium time decay chart in Figure 9.1, one may wonder what's wrong in closing the position on expiry day, since time decay will be maximum at that point? This, in turn, leads us back to the question — why do I close my positions one week before expiry?

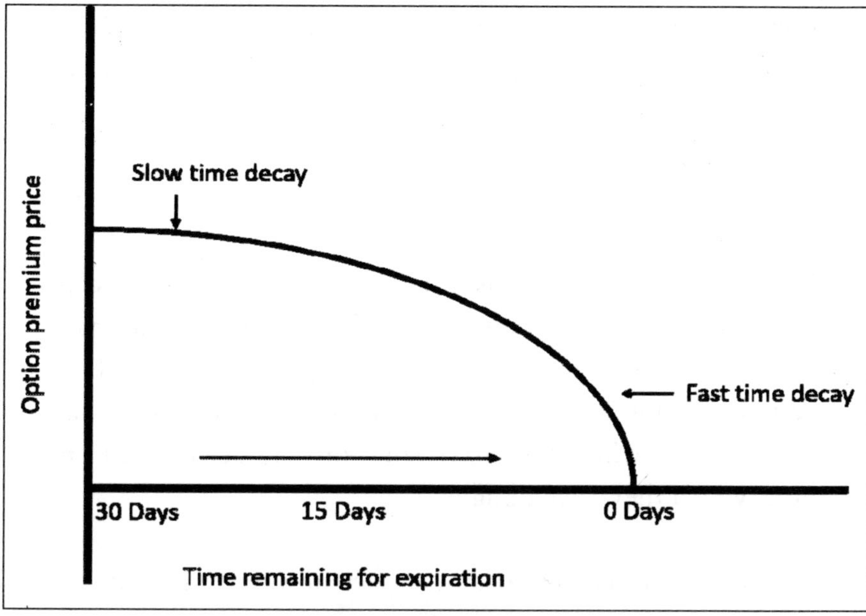

Figure 9.1: Time Decay of Option Premium

As an option seller, there is one more aspect you should be alert to — volatility. Volatility is usually high in the expiry week, and this is the reason I try to close my positions a week before expiry. Remember, option sellers do not like volatility because we only collect premiums and do not want market to become directional. If the market turns directional, you may lose in the last one week whatever premium you have earned till then. On the other hand, by closing one's position early you can gain most of the premium you may have let go by taking a fresh position for the next month expiry. As we can see in Figure 9.1, the longer the time left for the option's expiration, more will be the premium and more will be the profits. In other words, basically, the earlier we enter into a trade, higher the chances of making profits because of larger time value.

Stop Loss

In the context of options trading, stop loss is a concept which suggest that traders should close all their positions if they are in loss by a certain percentage of the capital invested. To close these positions, the trader may need to buy back options which they have sold, or may need to sell options which they have bought.

Stop loss is a very important aspect of any trade and you should follow it very strictly. For myself, I have made a rule that I will not lose more than 5% of margin money in any single trade. Since I usually open only one position in a month, so this also means that I don't want to lose more than 5% of margin money in any month.

We have already discussed how the Indian exchanges calculates SPAN, namely the initial margin, as well as the exposure margin. For example, if the margin money requirement to create an Iron Condor is ₹1,50,000, then I don't want to lose more than 5% of it, which translates to ₹7,500 in this case. So if my loss accumulates to ₹7,500, I would close this position and wait for the market conditions to become favorable again to enter into a fresh trade.

Now let's review some of my actual trades.

Trade-1: July 2020 Expiry

I usually initiate my option positions early. By early I mean more than 30 days ahead of the expiry. This way I get to collect higher premiums.

At the start of this trade, i.e. Trade-1, on 22 June, the closing price of SBIN was ₹187.70. SBIN had been range bound from quite some time and I anticipated that SBIN would not breach its 1SD values in July expiry. On 23 June, 1SD values for SBIN were ₹162 on the lower side and ₹223 on the higher side. So as per statistics, I was expecting SBIN to move between ₹162 and ₹223 till July expiry. With this market view, I started my July expiry trade positions on 23 June itself. My trade book is given in Table 9.1.

Table 9.1

Initiating the July 2020 Expiry Trade (Trade-1)

Date	*Company*	*Strike*	*Expiry*	*Side*	*Qty*	*Option Price*	*Net Amount (₹)*
23-06-2020	SBIN	140PE	30-07-2020	B	3,000	0.95	-2,850
23-06-2020	SBIN	160PE	30-07-2020	S	3,000	2.50	7,500
23-06-2020	SBIN	220CE	30-07-2020	S	3,000	4.60	13,800
23-06-2020	SBIN	250CE	30-07-2020	B	3,000	1.40	-4,200

To explain Table 9.1 clearly, I executed the following trades on 23 June 2020 for the underlying State Bank of India (SBIN) stock. Please note that the expiry date was 30 July 2020.

- Bought 1 lot SBIN@140PE at ₹0.95. Premium paid = 0.95 × 3,000 = ₹2,850.
- Sold 1 lot SBIN@160PE at ₹2.50. Premium received = 2.50 × 3,000 = ₹7,500.
- Sold 1 lot SBIN@220CE at ₹4.60. Premium received = 4.60 × 3,000 = ₹13,800.
- Bought 1 lot SBIN@250CE at ₹1.40. Premium paid = 1.40 × 3,000 = ₹4,200.

Please note that I had bought 140PE and 250CE to protect myself from any sudden market moves on either side. The total premium received from this trade was: –2,850 + 7,500, 13,800 – 4,200 = ₹14,250.

Why did I select strikes 160PE and 220CE to sell, you may ask. I did so as per Standard Deviation (1SD particularly), which we learnt about in Chapter 7.

On Friday 26 June, SBIN closed at ₹184.60 and things were not looking very optimistic for the stock. So, on Monday 29 June I became more aggressive on the sell side of CE and executed the additional adjustment trades shown in Table 9.2.

Table 9.2

Adjustments for July 2020 Expiry Trade (Trade-1)

Date	*Company*	*Strike*	*Expiry*	*Side*	*Qty*	*Price*	*Net Amount (₹)*
29-06-2020	SBIN	210CE	30-07-2020	S	3,000	3.20	9,600
29-06-2020	SBIN	220CE	30-07-2020	B	3,000	2.05	-6,150

To elaborate, I executed the following adjustment trades on 29 June 2020 for the underlying State Bank of India (SBIN). Please remember that the expiry date was 30 July 2020.

- Sold 1 lot SBIN@210CE at ₹3.20. Premium received = 3.20 × 3,000 = ₹9,600.
- Bought 1 lot SBIN@220CE at ₹2.05. Premium paid = 2.05 × 3,000 = ₹6,150.

By initiating the above two trades, I closed my 220CE trade completely. Remember, on 23 June I had sold this for a premium of ₹4.60 and now on 29 June I had bought it back. I got to keep ₹4.60 – ₹2.05 = ₹2.55 premium, which translated to 2.55 × 3,000 = ₹7,650. The selling of 210CE strike shows that I had more confidence that SBIN would not cross ₹210 in July expiry.

On 7 July, SBIN was striving to touch the ₹190 levels and it didn't look likely to go down any more from there. Accordingly, on the PE side I took a little more aggressive position on 8 July (*see* Table 9.3).

Table 9.3

Adjustments of 8 July (Trade-1)

Date	*Company*	*Strike*	*Expiry*	*Side*	*Qty*	*Option Price (₹)*	*Net Amount (₹)*
08-07-2020	SBIN	170PE	30-07-2020	S	3,000	2.05	6,150
08-07-2020	SBIN	160PE	30-07-2020	B	3,000	0.90	-2,700

To elaborate, I executed the following adjustment trades on 8 July 2020 for the underlying State Bank of India (SBIN). Please remember that the expiry date was 30 July 2020:

- Sold 1 lot SBIN@170PE at ₹2.05. Premium received = 3.20 × 3,000 = ₹6,150.
- Bought 1 lot SBIN@160PE at ₹0.90. Premium paid = 0.90 × 3,000 = ₹2,700.

With the above actions I effectively closed, i.e. squared off, my 160PE trade completely. On 23 June I had sold this strike at a premium of ₹2.50, and now I had bought it back on 8 July. I got ₹2.50 – 0.09 = ₹2.41 premium to keep, which translated to a total of 2.41 × 3,000 = ₹7,230. Selling 170PE showed that I had more than reasonable confidence that SBIN would not go below ₹170 in July expiry.

Following my rule of not being in the market in the last week of expiry, I subsequently closed all my positions on 24 July. SBIN was trading at ₹192 on that day (*see* Table 9.4).

Table 9.4

Exit Adjustments of 24 July (Trade-1)

Date	*Company*	*Strike*	*Expiry*	*Side*	*Qty*	*Price (₹)*	*Net Amount (₹)*
24-07-2020	SBIN	170PE	30-07-2020	B	3,000	0.40	-1,200
24-07-2020	SBIN	210CE	30-07-2020	B	3,000	1.40	-4,200
24-07-2020	SBIN	250CE	30-07-2020	S	3,000	0.10	300
24-07-2020	SBIN	140PE	30-07-2020	S	3,000	0.05	150

To elaborate, I executed the following adjustment trades on 24 July 2020 for the underlying State Bank of India (SBIN). Please note that the expiry date was 30 July 2020.

- Bought 1 lot SBIN@170PE at ₹0.40. Premium paid = 0.40 × 3,000 = ₹1,200.
- Bought 1 lot SBIN@210CE at ₹1.40. Premium paid = 1.40 × 3,000 = ₹4,200.
- Sold 1 lot SBIN@250CE at ₹3.20. Premium received = 0.10 × 3,000 = ₹300.
- Sold 1 lot SBIN@140PE at ₹0.05. Premium received = 0.05 × 3,000 = ₹150.

To summarize, Table 9.5 is my trade book for the July expiry trade, and it shows a profit of ₹16,200.

Table 9.5

Final Trade Book for July 2020 Expiry (Trade-1)

Date	*Company*	*Strike*	*Expiry*	*Side*	*Qty*	*Price (₹)*	*Net Amount (₹)*
23-06-2020	SBIN	140PE	30-07-2020	B	3,000	0.95	-2,850
23-06-2020	SBIN	160PE	30-07-2020	S	3,000	2.50	7,500
23-06-2020	SBIN	220CE	30-07-2020	S	3,000	4.60	13,800
23-06-2020	SBIN	250CE	30-07-2020	B	3,000	1.40	-4,200
29-06-2020	SBIN	210CE	30-07-2020	S	3,000	3.20	9,600
29-06-2020	SBIN	220CE	30-07-2020	B	3,000	2.05	-6,150
08-07-2020	SBIN	170PE	30-07-2020	S	3,000	2.05	6,150
08-07-2020	SBIN	160PE	30-07-2020	B	3,000	0.90	-2,700
24-07-2020	SBIN	170PE	30-07-2020	B	3,000	0.40	-1,200
24-07-2020	SBIN	210CE	30-07-2020	B	3,000	1.40	-4,200
24-07-2020	SBIN	250CE	30-07-2020	S	3,000	0.10	300
24-07-2020	SBIN	140PE	30-07-2020	S	3,000	0.05	150
Total P/L							16,200

Trade-2: August 2020 Expiry

As I have explained earlier, I start my option positions early. For the August expiry, which was on 27 August, I initiated my positions on 28 July itself.

On 27 July, SBIN was hovering around ₹188 and was looking strong. There had been occasions when it went down but, in a day or two it would bounce back to ₹190 levels. So, I was moderately bullish on SBIN and felt sure that it would not go down further.

Table 9.6

Initiating the August 2020 Expiry Trade (Trade-2)

Date	*Com pany*	*Strike*	*Expiry*	*Side*	*Qty*	*Price (₹)*	*Net Amount (₹)*
28-07-2020	SBIN	150PE	27-08-2020	B	3,000	1.60	-4,800
28-07-2020	SBIN	170PE	27-08-2020	S	3,000	5.20	15,600

Do you remember which hedging strategy we use as sellers if we are bullish on the market? The answer is bull put spread. I would encourage you to review the hedged strategies in Chapter 6 if you need to refresh your knowledge.

On 28 July, the lower 1SD level was close to ₹167. Accordingly, I decided to sell 170PE strike as shown in Table 9.6.

To explain Table 9.6 clearly, I executed the following trades on 28 July 2020 for the underlying State Bank of India (SBIN). Please note that the expiry date was 27 August 2020.

- Bought 1 lot SBIN@150PE at ₹1.60. Premium paid = 1.60 × 3,000 = ₹4,800.
- Sold 1 lot SBIN@170PE at ₹5.20. Premium received = 5.20 × 3,000 = ₹15,600.

I bought 150PE to protect myself from any sudden downtrend in SBIN.

Table 9.7

Trade-2: Adjustments of 31 July – Bear Call Spread

Date	*Company*	*Strike*	*Expiry*	*Side*	*Qty*	*Option Price (₹)*	*Net Amount (₹)*
31-07-2020	SBIN	220CE	27-08-2020	S	3,000	3.10	9,300
31-07-2020	SBIN	235CE	27-08-2020	B	3,000	1.60	-4,800

On 31 July, SBIN was trading at around ₹192, and appeared stable. Its 1SD level towards the upper side was ₹210, which I thought was too close to the strike considering all the positive news and volatility SBIN was exhibiting. So I decided to make a bear call spread by shorting 220CE and buying 235CE.

To explain Table 9.7 clearly, I executed the following trades on 31 July 2020 for the underlying State Bank of India (SBIN). Please note that expiry date was 27 August 2020.

- Sold 1 lot SBIN@220CE at ₹3.10 Premium received = ₹3.10 × 3,000 = ₹9,300.
- Bought 1 lot SBIN@235CE at ₹1.60. Premium paid = ₹1.60 × 3,000 = ₹4,800.

Can you understand why I made these trades? In effect, I made an Iron Condor part by part. Remember, **Iron Condor is nothing but the combination of a bull put spread and a bear call spread.**

Table 9.8

Trade-2: Adjustments of 10 August

Date	*Company*	*Strike*	*Expiry*	*Side*	*Qty*	*Price (₹)*	*Net Amount (₹)*
10-08-2020	SBIN	150PE	27-08-2020	S	3,000	0.20	600
10-08-2020	SBIN	170PE	27-08-2020	B	3,000	0.90	-2,700
10-08-2020	SBIN	235CE	27-08-2020	S	3,000	0.65	1,950
10-08-2020	SBIN	220CE	27-08-2020	B	3,000	1.85	-5,550

On 10 August, SBIN was trading close to ₹194. It was quite stable at those levels and the volatility became very low. Lower volatility means lower premiums. In fact, most of the premium had already eroded by that time, so I decided to close all my trades on 10 August itself.

To explain Table 9.8 clearly, I executed the following trades on 10 August 2020 for the underlying State Bank of India (SBIN). Please remember that the expiry date was 27 August 2020.

- Sold 1 lot SBIN@150PE at ₹0.20 Premium received = 0.20 × 3,000 = ₹600.
- Bought 1 lot SBIN@170PE at ₹0.90. Premium paid = 0.90 × 3,000 = ₹2,700.
- Sold 1 lot SBIN@235CE at ₹0.65. Premium received: 0.65 × 3,000 = ₹1,950.
- Bought 1 lot SBIN@220CE at ₹1.85. Premium paid: 1.85 × 3,000 = ₹5,500.

Table 9.9

Trade-2: Adjustments of 12 August

Date	*Company*	*Strike*	*Expiry*	*Side*	*Qty*	*Option Price (₹)*	*Net Amount (₹)*
12-08-2020	SBIN	220CE	27-08-2020	S	3,000	3.15	9,450
12-08-2020	SBIN	235CE	27-08-2020	B	3,000	1.25	-3,750

So, here I was with three weeks still left in August expiry and no open position in the market. I waited for another opportunity — and it came two day later. On 12 August, SBIN saw a huge up move and the price rose to ₹203. On the upside, SBIN had 1SD value of ₹221, so shorting 220CE looked like a good idea. Instead of an iron condor, I now decided to go with the bear call spread shown in Table 9.9.

To explain Table 9.9 clearly, I executed the following trades on 12 August 2020 for the underlying State Bank of India (SBIN). Please note that the expiry date was 27 August 2020.

- Sold 1 lot SBIN@220CE at ₹3.15. Premium received: ₹3.15 × 3,000 = ₹9,450.
- Bought 1 lot SBIN@235CE at ₹1.25. Premium paid: ₹1.25 × 3,000 = ₹3,750.

The rationale behind taking only the higher side position, or using a bear call spread, was that my previous experience had shown that when a sudden up trend reverses, it recedes even more quickly. So to be on the safe side I didn't create any put side position.

On 19 August, SBIN was trading at around ₹197 and I decided to close my positions (*see* Table 9.10).

In other words, I executed the following trades on 19 August 2020.

- Bought 1 lot SBIN@220CE at ₹1.05. Premium paid = ₹1.25 × 3,000 = ₹3,150.
- Sold 1 lot SBIN@235CE at ₹0.35. Premium received = ₹0.35 × 3,000 = ₹1,050.

Table 9.10

Trade-2: Adjustments of 19 August

Date	*Company*	*Strike*	*Expiry*	*Side*	*Qty*	*Option Price (₹)*	*Net Amount (₹)*
19-08-2020	SBIN	220CE	27-08-2020	B	3,000	1.05	-3,150
19-08-2020	SBIN	235CE	27-08-2020	S	3,000	0.35	1,050

Table 9.11

Trade-2: Final Trade Book

Date	*Com pany*	*Strike*	*Expiry*	*Side*	*Qty*	*Option Price (₹)*	*Net Amount (₹)*
28-07-2020	SBIN	150PE	27-08-2020	B	3,000	1.60	-4,800
28-07-2020	SBIN	170PE	27-08-2020	S	3,000	5.20	15,600
31-07-2020	SBIN	220CE	27-08-2020	S	3,000	3.10	9,300
31-07-2020	SBIN	235CE	27-08-2020	B	3,000	1.60	-4,800
10-08-2020	SBIN	150PE	27-08-2020	S	3,000	0.20	600
10-08-2020	SBIN	170PE	27-08-2020	B	3,000	0.90	-2,700
10-08-2020	SBIN	235CE	27-08-2020	S	3,000	0.65	1,950
10-08-2020	SBIN	220CE	27-08-2020	B	3,000	1.85	-5,550
12-08-2020	SBIN	220CE	27-08-2020	S	3,000	3.15	9,450
12-08-2020	SBIN	235CE	27-08-2020	B	3,000	1.25	-3,750
19-08-2020	SBIN	220CE	27-08-2020	B	3,000	1.05	-3,150
19-08-2020	SBIN	235CE	27-08-2020	S	3,000	0.35	1,050
Total P/L							13,200

Table 9.11 summarizes my trade book for the August expiry which shows a profit of ₹13,200.

Trade-3: September 2020 Expiry

Boosted by the confidence of two consecutive successful trades and substantial profits, I decided to initiate my trade for September expiry in mid-August itself. With a view that SBIN would not go down from its levels of 14 August, I made a bull put spread for the September expiry. SBIN had 1SD value of ₹183 on the lower side and it was trading

Table 9.12

Initiating the September 2020 Expiry Trade (Trade-3)

Date	*Company*	*Strike*	*Expiry*	*Side*	*Qty*	*Option Price (₹)*	*Net Amount (₹)*
14/08/2020	SBIN	160PE	24/09/2020	B	3,000	1.20	-3,600
14/08/2020	SBIN	180PE	24/09/2020	S	3,000	5.00	15,000

at around ₹197 on that day. As per the 1SD value, I decided to short 180PE. Also, to protect myself from any sudden downward move, I purchased 160PE (*see* Table 9.12).

In other words, I executed the following trades on 14 August 2020 for the underlying State Bank of India (SBIN). The expiry date was 24 September 2020.

- Bought 1 lot SBIN@160PE at ₹1.20. Premium paid: ₹1.20 × 3,000 = ₹3,600.
- Sold 1 lot SBIN@180PE at ₹5.0. Premium received: ₹5.00 × 3,000 = ₹15,000.

I initiated my September trade in August as the premiums then were really good because of the greater time value.

On 21 August, SBIN was trading around ₹200. Considering the fact that SBIN had not moved much beyond the ₹200 levels in the recent past and the 1SD value was ₹221 on the

Table 9.13

Trade-3: Adjustments of 25 August

Date	*Company*	*Strike*	*Expiry*	*Side*	*Qty*	*Option Price (₹)*	*Net Amount (₹)*
25/08/2020	SBIN	220CE	24/09/2020	S	3,000	5.00	15,000
25/08/2020	SBIN	230CE	24/09/2020	S	3,000	3.10	9,300
25/08/2020	SBIN	240CE	24/09/2020	B	6,000	1.75	-10,500

upper side, I made a bear call spread. Since option premiums were rich due to volatility, I became greedy and traded two lots though my bull put spread was still one lot trade only (*see* Table 9.13). This was a mistake.

To explain the trade clearly, on 25 August 2020 I executed the following trades for the underlying State Bank of India (SBIN). The expiry date was 24 September.

- Sold 1 lot SBIN@220CE at ₹5.0. Premium received: ₹5.0 × 3,000 = ₹15,000.
- Sold 1 lot SBIN@230CE at ₹5.0. Premium received: ₹3.10 × 3,000 = ₹9,300.
- Bought 2 lots SBIN@240CE at ₹1.75. Premium paid: ₹1.75 × 6,000 = ₹10,500.

On 28 August, and against all predictions, SBIN moved up to ₹225! Because my Iron Condor was unbalanced, with a 1-lot trade on the put side and a 2-lot trade on the call side,

Table 9.14

Trade-3: Adjustments of 28 August

Date	*Company*	*Strike*	*Expiry*	*Side*	*Qty*	*Option Price (₹)*	*Net Amount (₹)*
28/08/2020	SBIN	220CE	24/09/2020	B	3,000	12.00	-36,000
28/08/2020	SBIN	230CE	24/09/2020	B	3,000	6.50	-19,500
28/08/2020	SBIN	240CE	24/09/2020	S	6,000	4.00	24,000
28/08/2020	SBIN	160PE	24/09/2020	S	3,000	0.40	1,200
28/08/2020	SBIN	180PE	24/09/2020	B	3,000	0.90	-2,700

I was incurring more losses on the call side than the profit I was earning on the put side. On 28 August when my stop loss was hit, I exited from the September expiry trade (*see* Table 9.14).

Thus, the trades on 28 August were then as follows:

- Bought 1 lot SBIN@220CE at ₹12.00. Premium paid: ₹12.00 × 3,000 = ₹36,000.
- Bought 1 lot SBIN@230CE at ₹6.50. Premium paid: ₹6.50 × 3,000 = ₹19,500.
- Sold 2 lots SBIN@240CE at ₹4.00. Premium received: ₹4.00 × 6,000 = ₹24,000.
- Sold 1 lot SBIN@160PE at ₹0.40. Premium received: ₹0.40 × 3,000 = ₹1,200.
- Bought 1 lot SBIN@180PE at ₹0.90. Premium paid: ₹0.90 × 3,000 = ₹2,700.

Table 9.15

Trade-3: Final Trade Book

Date	*Company*	*Strike*	*Expiry*	*Side*	*Qty*	*Option Price (₹)*	*Net Amount (₹)*
14/08/2020	SBIN	160PE	24/09/2020	B	3,000	1.20	-3,600
14/08/2020	SBIN	180PE	24/09/2020	S	3,000	5.00	15,000
25/08/2020	SBIN	220CE	24/09/2020	S	3,000	5.00	15,000
25/08/2020	SBIN	230CE	24/09/2020	S	3,000	3.10	9,300
25/08/2020	SBIN	240CE	24/09/2020	B	6,000	1.75	-10,500
28/08/2020	SBIN	220CE	24/09/2020	B	3,000	12.00	-36,000
28/08/2020	SBIN	230CE	24/09/2020	B	3,000	6.50	-19,500
28/08/2020	SBIN	240CE	24/09/2020	S	6,000	4.00	24,000
28/08/2020	SBIN	160PE	24/09/2020	S	3,000	0.40	1,200
28/08/2020	SBIN	180PE	24/09/2020	B	3,000	0.90	-2,700
Total P/L							-7,800

To summarize, Table 9.15 shows my trade book for September expiry which shows a loss of ₹7,800. Why did I close my positions when my losses reached ₹7,800? That's because I was trading with a capital of ₹1,50,000 margin money and I was not willing to lose more than 5% (₹7,500) of this amount in one single trade.

Lessons Learnt from Trade-3 – the September Expiry Trade

I always try to learn something from my mistakes. What did I do wrong, or what could I have done differently? My September expiry losses taught me the following lessons:

- When SBIN was moving up I took a double position (2 lots) because premiums were high and I thought that would double my profits. In other words, I became greedy. I should not have done this in the first place. Thus, against 2 lots CE position, I had only 1 lot PE position. There was an imbalance — and when SBIN went up, I started making losses. Condors should always be balanced.

- I started my September trade too early, around 45 days before the September month expiry. From the Greeks chapter, we know that more the time to expiry, the higher would be the volatility, and hence higher the Vega. As an option approaches expiration and loses its time value; its Vega also goes down. So, the impact of a sudden uptrend in SBIN which came in August, was felt more in the September series options.

Key Takeaways from My Real-Life Trades

Learning a concept is very different from its application in a real trade. I have seen many people who paper traded for months and accumulated handsome profits on paper. But they were not very successful once they started to actually trade in real life. They made mistakes in calculations and also over-optimized their positions. They were either over optimistic about the market, or too fearful. They unnecessarily took bigger positions which actually led to bigger losses. It seemed as though all the systems they had developed over the many months of paper trading, or all the discipline they were able to maintain while paper trading, had all been forgotten.

There is a reason for all this — human emotions. Do you remember that in the initial chapters we had highlighted a stock market truth: "Greed, fear and panic are the most dangerous trinity working against traders?"

Making your option position bigger than warranted shows greed. The market will tempt you with seemingly quick money-making opportunities from time to time. Most of these opportunities will be risky trades. If such an opportunity is not aligned to your trading discipline or trading system, don't take it. Likewise, if some position doesn't need adjustment, don't adjust it. If your monthly trade target is being achieved by the current setup, do not alter your positions.

Summary

For trading I have always believed in the formula KISS – Keep It Simple, Stupid. The market is very complex and there is no fixed formula for market success. As my actual trades discussed above reveal, you are bound to have losses from time to time; so be ready for it. Losses should not derail your confidence in trading. Similarly, early success should not lead to overconfidence, or to taking unwarranted risks. Once you have mastered your emotions, trading will be far more profitable for you.

10

~

Roadmap for Earning Monthly Income from Options

We have now come to the last stage of our journey. Here I would like to share a few pointers about how you can evaluate when to enter a trade, when to exit, and when to make mid-trade adjustments. I have developed these guidelines by learning from my personal experience. Once you grow proficient in trading you may well arrive at some more guidelines for yourself. To start with, though, I feel the following would prove quite sufficient for most individual traders. The beauty of the stock market is that there is no definitive indication regarding its future directional movement. If there are factors supporting the market's upward trend, there will also be some negative factors waiting just round the corner which could bring down the market.

I am presenting below a roadmap about when to enter a trade, and how to manage it. This should be useful to you once you start your trading journey. I have explained this roadmap assuming that you want to trade using the Iron Condor strategy. Even if that is not your choice, I would suggest that you try to master Iron Condor. This will give you a deep insight into the dynamics of the market.

Entering a Trade

When you enter a trade, you need to look for certain indicators which should tell you whether the situation is suitable for you to initiate a new trade setup. All of the below mentioned indicators have been explained in detail in earlier chapters. Let's summarize these one by one.

Greek Values

When you try to trade the Iron Condor, you must check the Greek values of the overall setup. As explained earlier in the book, you can find live Greek values on the following websites:

- https://web.sensibull.com/
- https://opstra.definedge.com/

The Greek values we should be looking for would be as follows:

- Iron Condor being a Delta neutral strategy, the Delta should be 0, or near to 0. It represents that your view on the market is neutral.

- Theta should be positive. Theta represents time decay and in Iron Condor you earn money when premiums decay, hence Theta should be positive.

- Vega should be negative. Remember that in high volatility conditions, i.e. when Vega is positive. Iron Condor may give you losses unless you make adjustments to your position. Typically, there should be lower volatility for iron condors to succeed.
- Gamma, the rate of change of Delta, should be negative.

Selecting Strikes

Trade should be initiated based on 1SD on both sides. We have already discussed how you can calculate 1SD values in Chapter 7.

Checking for Major News

Check if any major news or event is imminent which may impact the market, whether positively or negatively. Or, maybe, there is an upcoming corporate result, or a dividend, or a bonus announcement about the stock which may increase its volatility. If any such event is forthcoming, try to avoid such a stock.

When to Initiate the Trade

Enter the trade only at 3:00 PM. That's because Theta will be decaying overnight, and you will thus start your position in profits the next day. Once you start the trade at 3:00 PM, there will be just thirty minutes of time remaining for the day which may not impact you much.

Check PCR

Check PCR before go entering a trade. PCR value will give you a hint about the upcoming market moves, and you can be prepared for that in advance. Remember: PCR >130 = overbought; PCR<60 = oversold; PCR~90 = bullish; PCR =100 = neutral.

Check Your Trade Positions Daily

Once the trade has been initiated, a daily check of your positions is essential. Here you need to be cautious as well. Monitoring your trade too often might lead you into over-adjusting your positions, which often hurts the overall result. You can't be looking at your trading terminal the whole day; equally, you must not react to each and every market move. Now, let's review what indicators you need to watch, and when.

Check Bollinger Bands

Once you have initiated your trade you should monitor Bollinger Bands on a daily basis, preferably on the daily chart. If you monitor the trade on an hourly chart, there will be so much market noise that you won't be able to determine the relevant market movement, since your position is multi-day and not multi-hour.

Watch Max OI

You should watch Max OI of CE and PE on a daily basis. This will tell you of any shift in market sentiment, and how might it play out in the upcoming days.

Watch Max Pain

As described earlier in Chapter 4, you should keep an eye on Max Pain on a daily basis. This may give you a hint as to where the market will be in the last week of expiry, and you can adjust your position accordingly.

Watch India VIX

Keep an eye on India VIX. This moves inversely to Nifty's movement. If Nifty goes down, VIX goes up, and *vice versa*. You can review Chapter 4 for details on India VIX. A high VIX may impact your Iron Condor positions. Iron Condor is a delta neutral positions and an increase in volatility is not good for it. Usually, the market is considered to be less volatile when India VIX remains between 14 to 17. This range of India VIX is ideal for trading iron condors. If VIX moves beyond 20, a trader should be ready to adjust the positions accordingly.

Check LTP

Check the underlying's price by 10:30 AM and then again 3:00 PM. Option positions are multi-day trades and checking the LTP very frequently throughout a day will not be of any benefit for you.

Managing Your Positions

This is the most important aspect of trading options. Most traders know how to enter a trade, but if you want to have a long and profitable innings in the derivatives market, you need to master the adjustment techniques which we have explored earlier in Chapter 8.

To reiterate, there are two rules of thumb regarding managing iron condors:

- For highly volatile stocks, like SBIN, we should adjust our positions only if the LTP of a stock comes within 5% of the strike price.
- For less volatile stocks, like ITC, we should adjust our positions only if the LTP of a stock comes within 3% of the strike price.

Let's refresh the significance of these percentages with the help of an example. Suppose the LTP of SBIN is ₹200, and you have initiated your Iron Condor for the current expiry as follows:

- Buy 160PE;
- Sell 180PE;
- Sell 220CE;
- Buy 240CE.

For this trade, let's quickly calculate how far the sell strikes are from the LTP:

- 220CE – ((220-200)/200) × 100 = 10%
- 180PE – ((180-200)/200) × 100 = –10%

In Chapter 8, we had calculated the percentage of upward movement of SBIN. Now let's calculate the percentage of its downward move. Suppose SBIN starts to move down and falls from ₹200 to ₹190, how much nearer is it from to the 180PE strike? It's now ((200-190)/200) × 100 = 5% to the 180PE strike. If SBIN continues to move downwards and breaches ₹190 then we must adjust our positions, since it is a volatile stock and often shows big movements.

You must, however, never try to over-optimize your trade positions. You need to work like a machine, i.e. without emotion, and only change or modify your position if it breaches above-mentioned percentage range.

Capital Required to Earn a Monthly Income from Options Trading

Now to a most important question. How much trading capital is needed to earn a monthly income of, say, ₹20,000 per month, from options trading.

The answer is — only ₹3.0 lakh!

Yes, that's it. Earlier, it used to be higher. In June 2020, however, SEBI announced reduced margin requirements for those who trade options using hedged positions, i.e. trades where your losses are defined. Anyone who has been a working professional for the last three or four years should have this much capital.

Now, if you earn ₹20,000 per month from a corpus of ₹3 lakh, that's a monthly return of more than 6%, or an annual return of more than 70%! At this rate, your initial capital of ₹3 lakh will double in less than 18 months.

Of course, you would be correct in wondering about the risks involved in this.

In India, derivatives trading is widely considered to be the riskiest type of trading, something which can even wipe out your entire capital in one go. This is true — but only up to a point because the risks involved can easily be avoided if you know what you are doing. In other words, you can greatly reduce the risks — and multiply your returns — through proper knowledge. Knowledge of the kind you have learnt in this book.

Summary

In this chapter I have provided concise guidelines that you need to check or cross-reference while entering a trade — and for adjusting a trade during its life. Once you start trading regularly, you will develop your own system and guidelines but, for now, these guidelines are quite adequate and you should try and follow them while trading. These guidelines will alert you in advance as to whether you need to make any adjustments to your trading positions.

11

~

Final Word

So that's it, then! You have now finished reading this book, and I would like to think that you have learnt something new and valuable from it.

We started with the basics of options, along with Greeks. Later, we explored some option selling strategies, and how one can make necessary adjustments to ongoing trades. We also saw how you can select our strikes using statistical tools. Finally, I provided a few guidelines which a trader needs to keep a tab on while trading.

I have learnt these things from my experience, and now through this book I am sharing my learning with fellow traders. I sincerely hope this book would prove beneficial to each of its readers.

All the best!